Praise for
Jennifer Kennedy Dean

"Jennifer supplied answers to questions I didn't know I had!"
—Bonnie Jones

"The details Jennifer provided about the setting of each parable made them come alive to me. As I saw each story unfold, it became more personal."
—Suzanne Free

"Jennifer Kennedy Dean's explanations of the parables made beautiful sense of stories that are sometimes difficult to understand, and she often evoked an emotional response at the same time."
—Landa Reynolds

"Jennifer opens the Lord's words so that everyone can understand. Her insight into prayer is powerful, and the parables speak to our needs."
—Carol Ann Holmes

"Jennifer is refreshing and encouraging! Her logical explanations of Jesus's interactions during His time on earth brought realism and humanity to His teachings."
—Karen O. Allen

OTHER NEW HOPE BOOKS AND PRODUCTS BY
JENNIFER KENNEDY DEAN

Secrets Jesus Shared Leader Kit

Heart's Cry: Principles of Prayer, Revised Edition

Live a Praying Life: Open Your Life to God's Power and Provision (Bible study)

Live a Praying Life Leader Kit

Fueled by Faith

The Life-Changing Power in the Name of Jesus (Bible study)

The Life-Changing Power in the Blood of Christ (Bible study)

Legacy of Prayer: A Spiritual Trust Fund for the Generations

Riches Stored in Secret Places: A Devotional Guide for Those Who Hunger After God

SECRETS JESUS SHARED

Secrets Jesus Shared

Kingdom Insights Revealed *Through* the Parables

JENNIFER KENNEDY DEAN

NEW HOPE
PUBLISHERS

Birmingham, Alabama

New Hope® Publishers
P. O. Box 12065
Birmingham, AL 35202-2065
www.newhopepublishers.com

Library of Congress Cataloging-in-Publication Data

Dean, Jennifer Kennedy.
  Secrets Jesus shared : kingdom insights revealed through the parables
/ Jennifer Kennedy Dean.
   p. cm.
  ISBN 978-1-59669-108-7 (soft cover)
  1. Jesus Christ—Parables. I. Title.
BT375.3.D43 2007
226.8'06—dc22
          2007003808

ISBN-10: 1-59669-108-5
ISBN-13: 978-1-59669-108-7

N074146 • 0807 • 7.1M1

DEDICATION

To my sons, Brantley, Kennedy, and Stinson.

And to my wonderful new daughter-in-law, Sara Campbell Dean.
We are so glad that Kennedy brought you into our family.

*"Walk in all the way that the LORD your God has commanded you,
so that you may live and prosper and prolong your days
in the land that you will possess."*
—Deuteronomy 5:33

TABLE OF CONTENTS

INTRODUCTION

In recent years, I have become particularly aware of the Hebrew context of the New Testament Scriptures. The more I study and research the cultural and historical settings of Jesus's words, the more depth I see in them. I realize that Jesus is often playful and lighthearted, not always stern and serious. Some of His best teaching is witty and funny. To know Him in His humorous aspects—to laugh with Him sometimes—frees me. Yet even His wit is eternally wise and life-giving.

I love to take the words of Jesus and let Him speak them to me now. To hear them from His heart to mine. To let them breathe. To let them sit in my heart until their full aroma has time to emerge. The parables are some of His most revealing words. More than stories, they are His description of the kingdom He rules and of which I am a citizen. He reveals so many aspects of His personality through the parables. His wit is on display, as is His wisdom. Rock-hard truth is spoken in gentle and genial love.

Some of my favorite words from Scripture are these: *"Let the word of Christ dwell in you richly"* (Colossians 3:16). As you study the parables of Jesus, I pray that His words will make their home in you. I pray that the richness of His words will permeate your heart and mind.

The Synoptic Gospels

The parables of Jesus are found in Matthew, Mark, and Luke. These are called the Synoptic Gospels, because they are so different from the Gospel of John. *Synoptic* means "viewing together," or seeing in the same way. The first three Gospels have much material in common and tend to see Jesus in the same way, whereas the Gospel of John contains different stories of Jesus and takes a somewhat different view of Him.

All of the Gospels were written many years after the Ascension of Jesus. The Gospel writers used research, oral history of the Christian community, and the memories of the people who had heard and known Jesus. The Gospels are not written as narratives. They are not intended to be history as much as synopses of the teachings of Jesus.

The most accepted theory is that Mark's Gospel was written first and that Matthew and Luke used Mark's Gospel as a source. Matthew and Luke had another common source that scholars refer to as *Q*. When something appears in Matthew and Luke, but not in Mark, then it is assumed to have come from Q. Luke had yet another source that neither Mark nor Matthew seemed to have used, and it is referred to as *L*. Some people think that L was the Apostle Paul.

Sometimes when the same parable is told in different Gospels, it is told a little differently or the setting is described differently. When you realize that Jesus taught for hours, even days, at a time, and that He taught in different settings and to different audiences, you can easily see why there are different versions. Of course, He would tell variations of the same parable in different settings. Or He would tell a very similar parable but make a different point. It is not at all surprising that there are different versions of the same parable.

When I chose which version of a certain parable to concentrate on for this study, I used the research of linguists to consider which version seems to maintain the most authentic Hebrew or Aramaic grammar and syntax. Jesus did not speak His parables in Greek. They were translated into Greek. Another of my criteria was that I chose to use the version with the most detail.

How Were Jesus's Parables Preserved?

In this study, the Hebrew way of learning will be explained. Memorization was the way learning occurred in Jesus's time because people did not have personal copies of the sacred teaching. The Talmud, the oral law, was not written down until several hundred years after Jesus. In His time, the only way to know Talmud was by precise memorization. The Hebrew culture was built around verbatim memorization. It was as natural to them as reading is to us. They trusted memorization far more than they trusted writing. Talmud was not written because they feared that once it was written, scribal errors in copying would occur, and error would begin to creep in.

Think of something that you know verbatim—maybe the Pledge of Allegiance. Because you know each word so well and have heard it and repeated it so many times, if you hear someone say the wrong word, you immediately know it. However, if you read it, your brain might see what it thinks it will see. There may be an error, and you might not see it.

The form in which Jesus's parables were preserved and repeated was very reliable. Any person repeating any teaching of Jesus would have felt heavy obligation to repeat it exactly.

We do not have the original manuscripts of the New Testament. The manuscripts we have are written in Greek. Scholars are more and more convinced that the originals, if we could ever find them, were not written in Greek, but in Aramaic or Hebrew. Certainly the original language of the writers was not Greek. Even if they did write in Greek, they were thinking in Hebrew.

Each time an older version of any manuscript is discovered, it is noted that little changes have been made—usually to keep up with changes in the Greek language as it evolved. Sometimes it is discovered that little things have been added in later manuscripts that were not in earlier manuscripts. New discoveries do not change the revealed truths, but only add new depth. The history of Scripture, God's written Word, is a fascinating and ongoing study.

I am confident that the Holy Spirit has been and is watching over the Word of God and keeping theological error from it. Jesus's parables would be the most closely and carefully preserved of all the words Jesus spoke. The Jewish people were used to being taught by parables, and the very form of the parable was meant to make it easy to memorize.

I hope that you enjoy this study of the parables of Jesus and that Jesus Himself speaks to you truth that transforms your life.

THE SECRETS OF THE KINGDOM

DAY 1

"*The secret of the kingdom of God has been given to you*" (Mark 4:11). Jesus spoke these words to His twelve disciples on a given day in history, and He is still speaking to His disciples in present tense. The secrets of the kingdom have been given to *you*. You are so honored and so beloved in the kingdom that the King has opened His heart to you and has disclosed to you His secrets. He has revealed to you the *"deep and hidden things"* that belong only to Him (Daniel 2:22).

The secrets of the kingdom have been *given* to you. The Greek word translated "given" has several implications. It means to give as a gift, to bestow upon. It can also mean to furnish or provide necessities. It can mean to entrust or commit to one's care. It means to give from oneself, to give forth, to give out. The secrets have been freely given to you as a gift. The secrets furnish you with all you need for kingdom living. They have been entrusted to your care. They have been given to you from the very heart of the King. The tense of the verb *given* means it is an action completed in the past having present results. The secrets have already been given to you, and the effect of that gift is being worked out in you daily. You are comprehending it more each day.

In a television ad for a certain pasta sauce, as each ingredient is mentioned, the announcer says, "It's in there." The Scripture says the same to us about the gift of the secrets of the kingdom. Pointing to your heart, you can rightly say, "It's in there."

Who knows your secrets? Do you share your secrets with strangers or even acquaintances? Secrets are for those closest to us, those whom we trust. The deeper the secret, the more intimacy is involved in its sharing. The King has brought you into His inner circle. He holds nothing back from you. He delights in letting you know what is in His heart. He is pleased to disclose to you the things that He alone knows. What intimacy! What love! What privilege!

WEEK ONE

Read Daniel 2:22.

> *"He reveals deep and hidden things;*
> *he knows what lies in darkness,*
> *and light dwells with him."*
> —**Daniel 2:22**

Now read I Corinthians 2:9–11.

> *"No eye has seen,*
> *no ear has heard,*
> *no mind has conceived*
> *what God has prepared for those who love him"*—
>
> *but God has revealed it to us by his Spirit.*
> *The Spirit searches all things, even the deep things of God.*
> —1 Corinthians 2:9–11

When you line up these Old Testament and New Testament Scriptures (Daniel 2:22 and I Corinthians 2:9–11), what do you hear the Lord saying to you about His deep and hidden things? Does He want to keep them hidden?

Read Psalm 25:14.

> *The LORD confides in those who fear him.*
> —Psalm 25:14

Now read John 15:15.

> *"I no longer call you servants, because a servant does not know his master's business. Instead, I have called you friends, for everything that I learned from my Father I have made known to you."*
> —John 15:15

When you line up these Old Testament and New Testament Scriptures (Psalm 25:14 and John 15:15), what do you hear the Lord saying to you about what He wants to disclose to you?

The statement Jesus made about the secrets of the kingdom—*"The secret of the kingdom of God has been given to you"* (Mark 4:11)—was made in response to a question the disciples asked about the parables. According to Matthew 13, the disciples wanted to know why He was teaching in parables. His response indicated the secrets of the kingdom are embedded in His parables.

As you join me in this study of the parables of Jesus, let's ask the Holy Spirit to reveal deep truths from His Word that will give us more wisdom and insight about how to live fully in His kingdom.

WEEK ONE

DAY 2

The advent of the long-awaited Messiah was meticulously timed and scrupulously prepared. Nothing was incidental. Every detail had been strategically planned since before the world began. It was no coincidence that the Hebrew nation and the Jewish religion formed the backdrop against which the greatest parable was enacted. It was no accident that it happened when the proud Jewish nation was subject to the harsh rule of Rome. It was not by chance that He came into a setting where the faith of the patriarchs had morphed into a rigid, oppressive set of regulations.

Jewish Backdrop

The Jewishness of Jesus is an essential aspect of the revelation. Jesus was a Hebrew, born of Hebrews. He was a Jew among Jews. His lineage was the framework that gave the story its texture. To understand His parables, we have to understand their context.

During the years of Jesus's ministry, He was recognized as a rabbi. The designation of *rabbi* was specific. It meant something definite. It was not a generic form of address, such as *sir* or *mister*. It meant a teacher of stature and learning—one who interpreted the words of Torah with special insight. A rabbi was respected and honored. To become learned enough to be a rabbi was a strenuous pursuit, one that required very high intelligence and great discipline and tenacity. Jesus was addressed as rabbi by a variety of people: His disciples (Luke 7:40), a lawyer (Matthew 22:35), a rich man (Matthew 19:16), the crowds (Luke 12:13), Pharisees (Luke 19:39), and Sadducees (Luke 20:27–28). Your version of the Bible might translate the word as "teacher" or "master." The Hebrew word is *rav*. When His contemporaries addressed Him, they did not speak Greek. They spoke Aramaic with much Hebrew sprinkled in, or they spoke a form of Hebrew that was less structured than the formal Hebrew in which the Holy Scriptures were written. His contemporaries called Him *Rav Yeshua*—Rabbi Jesus.

The Jewish religion had not only the written Word (Torah), but also the oral law and the many interpretations of the rabbis and sages throughout their history (Talmud). In Jesus's day, Talmud was not written down. It had to be memorized. Memorization in the Jewish culture was exact and word-for-word. One could not summarize the words of a rabbi. They had to be quoted exactly.

People did not have scrolls in their homes. The scrolls that contained the Hebrew Scriptures were kept at the synagogue. Because memorization was paramount in Jewish culture and because knowledge of Torah was so important, Hebrew children were trained from their earliest years how to memorize. The early games that parents played with their young children were games that would prepare them to memorize.

All Jewish children memorized the first five books of the Bible and went to school until they were 12 years old. After the age of 12, only the most advanced ones continued in their education. Those who showed extreme ability and who stood out far above the other students might then leave home to study with a rabbi, or become a disciple. These rabbis and disciples spent day and night studying and reflecting upon Torah and Talmud. They memorized it, they debated it, they analyzed it, they dissected it, they taught it, and they preached it. A disciple, when he was fully taught, might then become a rabbi.

Rabbi Jesus

When Rabbi Jesus taught, other rabbis and scholars—men whose whole lives consisted of studying and teaching and who listened to numerous teachers year after year—were astounded at His teaching. Astounded! Left speechless. *"The Jews were amazed and asked, 'How did this man get such learning without having studied?'"* (John 7:15). When the writer of the Gospel of John used the term *the Jews* in his Gospel, he was referring to the leaders. The leading scholars and opinion shapers were amazed. They were all the more amazed because He had such learning without having studied with a rabbi. (I explored this in great detail in my Bible study titled, *The Life-Changing Power in the Name of Jesus.*)

Rabbi Jesus, His teaching shows, had mastered not only the written Word, the Holy Scriptures, but He also was fully versed in oral law. He was very observant in His dress and His behavior. We sometimes have the idea that He flaunted tradition for the sake of making His point. He did break oral law a few times for certain purposes, but He was ready to explain His deviation on the authority of Holy Scripture. He didn't do so mindlessly. He challenged the leaders in their public debates on points of interpretation, basing His arguments solely on Scripture. His teaching used forms, phrasing, and references that were familiar to those listening, and He used many traditional rabbinical methods. He debated in the same style that the scholars and sages of His time employed.

The Rabbi-Disciple Relationship

Like Rabbi Jesus, most rabbis traveled from town to town and from village to village, teaching. Like Rabbi Jesus, they taught in homes, outdoors, or in the synagogue. Like Rabbi Jesus, they each had a group of disciples who traveled with them, not only acquiring knowledge from the rabbi, but also learning from his life. A rabbi might have a large group of disciples who accompanied him, but a hand-selected few from that group were his elite. These are the ones who stayed with him day and night and who were the recipients of his innermost thoughts and ideas. The larger group of disciples might follow for a while and then return home. Their ranks changed from day to day. But those in the inner circle devoted their lives to this particular rabbi.

The rabbi-disciple relationship was referred to as father and son or, sometimes, master and slave. Disciples called their rabbis "father," and a rabbi called his disciples "sons." The rabbi took the place of the father. The Talmud taught that if a disciple's father and rabbi were both in trouble, the disciple was obligated to help his rabbi first.

Having the visiting rabbi in your home was a great honor. A hundred years or more before Jesus walked the earth, Rabbi Yose ben Yoezer had declared, "Let your home be a meeting place for the sages, and cover yourself with the dust of their feet, and drink in their words thirstily." To cover yourself with the dust of a rabbi's feet meant to sit at his feet to learn from him. However, disciples who traveled with their rabbi, following him from town to town, would soon be covered with the dust that his feet kicked up on the dusty, unpaved roads upon which they walked. It was their badge of honor to be covered with the dust of their rabbi's feet. It proved that they were one of the inner circle. It proved how closely they followed him (David Bivin, *New Light on the Difficult Words of Jesus*).

Consider the number of times that the Gospels describe Jesus teaching the crowds in someone's private home. Think about how many times the Gospels tell about Jesus teaching on a hillside or from a boat or in a field. Remember Mary being commended by Jesus for sitting at His feet. Rabbi Jesus lived and conducted His teaching ministry according to the customs of rabbis of His time.

In what language did Jesus speak?

_____

_____

What was the religious background of most of His audience?

_____

_____

_____

_____

_____

When Jesus referred to the Scripture, to what was He referring?

_____

_____

_____

_____

_____

Why did Jesus travel from place to place and stay in the homes of other people?

_____

_____

_____

_____

_____

_____

Why do we often see Jesus portrayed in the Gospels as having crowds around Him?

_____

_____

_____

_____

_____

_____

_____

J esus's invitation to discipleship is framed in these words:

> *"Come to me, all you who are weary and burdened, and I will give*
> *you rest. Take my yoke upon you and learn from me, for I am gentle*
> *and humble in heart, and you will find rest for your souls. For my*
> *yoke is easy and my burden is light."*
> —Matthew 11:28–30

A Rabbi's Yoke

In the rabbinical system, there were different schools of rabbinical thought, and these schools, or ways of approaching interpretation of the Torah, were called "yokes." To become a disciple of one rabbi or another was to take that particular rabbi's yoke upon your neck. Rabbis debated one another, and their disciples debated the disciples of other rabbis. They wore different "yokes."

When Jesus's contemporaries heard Him invite them to take His yoke upon them, there was no confusion about what He meant. *"Take my yoke upon you and learn **from** me,"* He said. A disciple did not learn *about* his rabbi. He learned *from* his rabbi. A disciple was not a casual learner; rather, he was one who left everything else in order to follow his rabbi day and night. He gained far more than knowledge from his rabbi. He absorbed his rabbi's life. A disciple learned from his rabbi a way of thinking and living: He listened to his rabbi; he discussed and debated with his rabbi; he ate as his rabbi ate; he slept as his rabbi slept; and he used his rabbi's phrases and speech patterns. When he quoted his rabbi, he quoted verbatim. He took no liberties with his master's words. As much as was possible, the rabbi reproduced himself in the disciple. A disciple followed his rabbi so closely, he, figuratively speaking, was covered with the dust of his rabbi's feet.

A disciple's life required sacrifice. Peter said, *"We have left all we had to follow you!"* (Luke 18:28). Jesus challenged those who would be His disciples first to count the cost. *"Suppose one of you wants to build a tower. Will he not first sit down and estimate the cost to see if he has enough money to complete it? For if he lays the foundation and is not able to finish it, everyone who sees it will ridicule him, saying, 'This fellow began to build and was not able to finish'"* (Luke 14:28–30). He made it clear that to be His disciple would cost a person everything.

After counting the cost, then count the reward. Jesus challenged those who sought to be His disciples to count the reward also: *"And everyone who has left houses or brothers or sisters or father or mother or children or fields for my sake will receive a hundred times as much and will inherit eternal life"* (Matthew 19:29). *"If you hold to my teaching, you are really my disciples. Then you will know the truth, and the truth will set you free"* (John 8:31–32).

When the benefit far outweighs the cost, we call it gain. Discipleship will cost you everything you have, but it will gain you even more.

> *Peter said to him, "We have left all we had to follow you!"*
> *"I tell you the truth," Jesus said to them, "no one who has left home or wife or brothers or parents or children for the sake of the kingdom of God will fail to receive many times as much in this age and, in the age to come, eternal life."*
> —Luke 18:28–30

Rabbi Jesus said that His yoke is easy and His burden light.

Other rabbis made the Law heavier and heavier, more and more burdensome. They added to the Law by requiring behaviors that were beyond anything the Law asked. Jesus described it this way: *"They tie up heavy burdens and lay them on men's shoulders"* (Matthew 23:4 NASB). The Greek word translated "burden" is the same one used when Jesus said, *"My burden is light"* (Matthew 11:30). The word can mean either something owed like an invoice or something carried, such as the cargo of a ship.

Paul referred to the yoke that had been put upon disciples throughout Israel's history. Addressing those who would require new Christian converts to follow unnecessary rules, Paul said, *"Now then, why do you try to test God by putting on the necks of the disciples a yoke that neither we nor our fathers have been able to bear?"* (Acts 15:10).

No other rabbi would declare that his yoke was easy or his burden light. They were more likely to boast of the heaviness of their burden. Jesus's call to an easy yoke and a lightened burden was unusual. His promise to give rest might have called to His listeners' mind God's promise to Moses: *"My Presence will go with you, and I will give you rest"* (Exodus 33:14). Jesus was inviting people to yoke themselves to Him, and, because His strength would be the driving force, under His yoke, they would find rest. His presence with them would give them rest.

As you move further into this study of the secrets of the kingdom hidden in Jesus's parables, the invitation to you is to take His yoke upon you and learn from Him. The secrets hidden in the parables are for the inner circle of disciples. Would you choose to accept that invitation from Rabbi Jesus?

Read Matthew 11:28–30, and let the Holy Spirit make the words of Jesus personal to you. Let Him speak this invitation to you in present tense.

- *"Come to me, _____ (Put your name here.), all you who are weary [fatigued, overworked] and burdened [loaded down],"*

  Write out how this phrase describes you. Write how you are weary and burdened.

  _____

  _____

  _____

  _____

- *"and I will give you rest [refreshment]."*

  Write how your heart responds to this invitation of rest:

  _____

  _____

  _____

  _____

- *"Take my yoke upon you"*

   Restate this invitation in words more relevant to you, then write your response to this invitation.

   _____

   _____

   _____

   _____

   _____

- *"and learn from me,"*

   Write what you want to learn from Him.

   _____

   _____

   _____

   _____

- *"for I am gentle and humble in heart,"*

   When you see that Jesus is gentle and humble, what does that mean to you?

   _____

   _____

   _____

   _____

   _____

- *"and you will find rest for your souls."*

How do you respond to this promise?

_____

_____

_____

_____

- *"For my yoke is easy and my burden is light."*

Take some time to consider His yoke, and then thank Him for it. What yoke will His yoke be replacing in your life?

_____

_____

_____

_____

Emergence: Mikveh

At the age of 30, Jesus emerged on the public stage. He came to John the Baptizer, the preeminent preacher at the time, for *mikveh* [pronounced mick-vah]. Mikveh was part of Jewish tradition since God had first given the instructions for the priesthood. Mikveh was a ceremony in which the person submerged himself under water and then came back up again. It had many applications, one of which was the initiation of a priest into his priestly duties. A bride performed mikveh in preparation for her wedding. Anyone who came into contact with anything thought unclean performed mikveh as part of their cleansing. Mikveh had a twofold meaning: (1) a cleansing and (2) a dying to old and rising to new. The symbolism was that as the person went under the water, his breath was stolen away; as he came up again, his breath was restored to him. Mikveh was a familiar practice among the Jewish people.

Mikveh was also commonly used as a symbol of having embraced the teaching of a certain rabbi or sage. A person was said to "mikveh into" that teacher, thereby fully associating with that teaching. For example, Paul wrote that all the nation of Israel was *"baptized* [mikveh] *into Moses"* when they passed through the Red Sea (1 Corinthians 10:2). They fully embraced the leadership and teaching of Moses. In 1 Corinthians 1:10–17, Paul addressed the issues that came from people claiming to be followers of certain teachers. Paul asked, "Were you baptized [mikveh] into my name?" He was reminding them that they did not mikveh into any one teacher, but their mikveh was into Christ. He said to the Romans, *"Or don't you know that all of us who were baptized* [mikveh] *into Christ Jesus were baptized* [mikveh] *into his death?"* (Romans 6:3). The role of baptism, or mikveh, was well understood by the Jewish people.

Message: Repent, the Kingdom Is Here

Only after Jesus had participated in a mikveh—had been ceremonially initiated into His role as priest—did He begin to preach publicly. And what did He preach? *"From that time on Jesus began to preach, 'Repent, for the kingdom of heaven is near'"* (Matthew 4:17). What had John the Baptizer preached? *"In those days John the Baptist came, preaching in the Desert of Judea and saying, 'Repent, for the kingdom of heaven is near'"* (Matthew 3:1–2). Publicly, Jesus fully associated Himself with the message of John, who had been sent to prepare the ground for the seed of the gospel. John's protest to Jesus's baptism was that he, John, was Jesus's disciple, not the other way around. He was the voice *"calling in the desert, 'Prepare the way for the Lord'"* (Matthew 3:3).

John and Jesus preached the same message: Repent, because the kingdom of heaven is near. John was the *voice* calling in the wilderness, but Jesus was the *Word* made flesh. John was the messenger. Jesus was the Message.

The message Jesus preached, taught, and lived out remained the same throughout His public ministry. *"**From that time on** Jesus began to preach, 'Repent, for the kingdom of heaven is near'"* (Matthew 4:17; bold added). No matter what form the message took—whether demonstration or parable or exposition of the Torah or answer to questions—the message was the same from first day to last: *"Repent, for the kingdom of heaven is near."*

The Hebrew word that Jesus would likely have used for *repent* means to turn, to change the way of thinking. "Change your mind," says it partially. But it is not just "change your opinion" or "change your beliefs." More accurately, it means to "reorient your thinking" or "refocus your attention."

Repent is the first word of the message, and it was spoken as a strong command. Repent! Why? Repent *because* the kingdom of heaven is near. The language does not mean the kingdom is coming, is about to come, or is in the process of coming. Rather, it means the kingdom of heaven *has come.* The kingdom of heaven is here. The King James Version of the Bible and the *New American Standard Bible* both translate *near* as "at hand." The phrase *at hand* means right here, within reach. Right here for the taking. Just reach out and grab hold.

The message is this: Reorient your thinking and refocus your view because the kingdom of heaven is right here for the taking. Why would we need to reorient and refocus because the kingdom has come? The kingdom of God is invisible. It is not made of earth stuff. If we have our attention and our focus on that which is material and physical, we will not see the kingdom. *"So we fix our eyes not on what is seen, but on what is unseen. For what is seen is temporary, but what is unseen is eternal"* (2 Corinthians 4:18).

Mark the phrases in the following passages that indicate that the kingdom of God is not visible.

Once, having been asked by the Pharisees when the kingdom of God would come, Jesus replied, "The kingdom of God does not come with your careful observation, nor will people say, 'Here it is,' or 'There it is,' because the kingdom of God is within you."
—Luke 17:20–21

In reply Jesus declared, "I tell you the truth, no one can see the kingdom of God unless he is born again."
—John 3:3

Jesus said, "My kingdom is not of this world. If it were, my servants would fight to prevent my arrest by the Jews. But now my kingdom is from another place."
—John 18:36

For the kingdom of God is not a matter of eating and drinking, but of righteousness, peace and joy in the Holy Spirit.
—Romans 14:17

For the kingdom of God is not a matter of talk but of power.
—1 Corinthians 4:20

The words "once more" indicate the removing of what can be shaken—that is, created things—so that what cannot be shaken may remain.
    Therefore, since we are receiving a kingdom that cannot be shaken, let us be thankful, and so worship God acceptably with reverence and awe, for our "God is a consuming fire."
—Hebrews 12:27–29

Mark the phrases in the following passages that indicate that the kingdom of God has come.

"But seek first his kingdom and his righteousness, and all these things will be given to you as well."
—Matthew 6:33

"I tell you the truth: Among those born of women there has not risen anyone greater than John the Baptist; yet he who is least in the kingdom of heaven is greater than he. From the days of John the Baptist until now, the kingdom of heaven has been forcefully advancing, and forceful men lay hold of it."
—Matthew 11:11–12

"But if I drive out demons by the Spirit of God, then the kingdom of God has come upon you."
—Matthew 12:28

For he has rescued us from the dominion of darkness and brought us into the kingdom of the Son he loves, in whom we have redemption, the forgiveness of sins.
—Colossians 1:13–14

To him who loves us and has freed us from our sins by his blood, and has made us to be a kingdom and priests to serve his God and Father—to him be glory and power for ever and ever!
—Revelation 1:5–6

Although Jesus taught and proclaimed that the kingdom of God had come and was present, there is an aspect of the kingdom that is to come. Most theologians recognize the *now* and the *not yet* aspects of the kingdom. It will be clothed in the created order when Christ makes His triumphant return. The kingdom sometimes also refers to our eternal dwelling place in the presence of God. But for the most part, Jesus's teaching pointed to the kingdom of God as present among humans. His message was that the long-awaited salvation, which to the Hebrew mind was inextricably one with the kingdom, has arrived on earth in His person—the person of Jesus. The kingdom of heaven has invaded earth. The kingdom of God has entered the environment of earth through the eternal Word made flesh. Wahoo! I know that is not a sophisticated word, but it was the only word I could think of to express the excitement of such a revelation. So I'll just say it again: Wahoo!

Redirection of Expectations: Kingdom of God

Jewish expectation of the kingdom of God entailed a physical King-Messiah who would defeat their oppressors and establish them in a land with a geographical location. Moses being the former redeemer, the latter Redeemer is a name often used for this Messiah. He was also referred to as the Promised One or the Prophet. The title *Prophet* is based on Moses's words: *"The LORD your God will raise up for you a prophet like me from among your own brothers. You must listen to him"* (Deuteronomy 18:15).

The kingdom of God and the kingdom of heaven are two ways of saying the same thing. Where Mark and Luke use the phrase *kingdom of God,* Matthew usually uses *kingdom of heaven.* Matthew was writing primarily to a Jewish audience. Among the Jews, using God's name was prohibited because it was too holy to pronounce, so the word *heaven* often substituted for *God*—or, really, *Yahweh,* the unpronounceable name. In order to avoid even the accidental breaking of the commandment not to take the name of the Lord in vain, the oral law dictated that the name not be spoken or written. Mark's and Luke's audiences included Gentiles, who would not have understood the word *heaven* in the same way.

The kingdom of God was part of Jewish thought from the time of Abraham. The land of Canaan, Palestine in Jesus's time, a land located on earth in a specific geographical area, was the kingdom. It could be identified on a map or described by longitude and latitude. It was a place in the universe of space and time. In Jesus's time, their land was under the rule of Rome. In their own land, they were under the rule of a pagan nation. How they longed for the Messiah to appear and defeat their captors and restore the kingdom.

When Jesus started talking about the kingdom, He was speaking directly to the heart of the Hebrew nation. He was hitting the high note.

Take time to read through these representative verses, highlighting the terms *the kingdom,* *the kingdom of God,* **and** *the kingdom of heaven.* **This will give you a visual of the thread and the defining theme of Jesus's message.**

> *Jesus went throughout Galilee, teaching in their synagogues, preaching the good news of the kingdom, and healing every disease and sickness among the people.*
> —**Matthew 4:23**

> *Jesus went through all the towns and villages, teaching in their synagogues, preaching the good news of the kingdom and healing every disease and sickness.*
> —**Matthew 9:35**

> *"As you go, preach this message: 'The kingdom of heaven is near.'"*
> —**Matthew 10:7**

> *"And this gospel of the kingdom will be preached in the whole world."*
> —**Matthew 24:14**

> *But he said, "I must preach the good news of the kingdom of God to the other towns also, because that is why I was sent."*
> —**Luke 4:43**

After this, Jesus traveled about from one town and village to another, proclaiming the good news of the kingdom of God.
—Luke 8:1

And he sent them out to preach the kingdom of God and to heal the sick.
—Luke 9:2

He welcomed them and spoke to them about the kingdom of God, and healed those who needed healing.
—Luke 9:11

"Heal the sick who are there and tell them, 'The kingdom of God is near you.'"
—Luke 10:9

After his suffering, he showed himself to these men and gave many convincing proofs that he was alive. He appeared to them over a period of forty days and spoke about the kingdom of God.
—Acts 1:3

The kingdom of God was the crux of Jesus's message, and He had to completely redefine the concept. They had to unlearn everything they thought they knew. To teach is one thing, but to *unteach* takes a skill and brilliance and understanding few have.

DAY 4

To recap, the kingdom is fully in effect and has always been so in the heavenly realms, where God sits enthroned. The kingdom will be coming at some time in the future in a physical manifestation. But that very kingdom—with its power and authority—has come to earth through Jesus. The kingdom of God, with its power, authority, and resources, is available in the present-tense life of those in whom Jesus dwells.

Eternal Kingdom of God

The kingdom did not come into being when Jesus came to earth and began His ministry. The kingdom has always been in existence. Before the Word became flesh, the kingdom was operating. The kingdom is eternal—it has no beginning, and it has no end. The kingdom of God is the reign or the rule of God. Wherever God is, there the kingdom is, because God rules. God *is* the kingdom.

Doesn't God exist everywhere? Isn't He everywhere all the time? So isn't the kingdom always present? Well, yes and no.

God is indeed present and sovereign everywhere all the time. Everything that exists, exists because He created it and maintains it and wills for it to exist.

> *The earth is the LORD's, and everything in it,*
> *the world, and all who live in it.*
> —Psalm 24:1

> *The heavens are yours, and yours also the earth;*
> *you founded the world and all that is in it.*
> —Psalm 89:11

In His sovereignty and according to His purpose and by His deliberate plan, He has chosen to leave humans free to experience His kingdom, through His presence, or not.

"The highest heavens belong to the LORD, but the earth he has given to man" (Psalm 115:16). He can give it to man only if it belongs to Him and is His to give. And this does not mean that He has backed out and relinquished ownership, but that He has entrusted the earth to mankind.

He has left mankind free to choose His kingdom. In so doing, He has not relinquished His sovereignty. He rules over the affairs of mankind and allows for the choices and responses they make. At any given moment, we can choose to experience the kingdom of God.

Also, for this period, Satan has a realm over which he rules, although his rule is strictly limited by God and is overcome as God's kingdom authority is exercised. His is a tenuous authority, but still he has been given a realm in which he rules for a specified time. Several times in John's Gospel, Jesus refers to Satan as *"the prince of this world"* (John 12:31; 14:30; 16:11). Paul describes Satan as *"the ruler of the kingdom of the air, the spirit who is now at work in those who are disobedient"* (Ephesians 2:2). During the intensive temptation of Jesus following His baptism, Satan offered Jesus all the kingdoms of the world: *"Again, the devil took him to a very high mountain and showed him all the kingdoms of the world and their splendor. 'All this I will give you,' he said, 'if you will bow down and worship me'"* (Matthew 4:8–9). In order to offer them, they had to be his to give.

The kingdom of God will always, without fail, overpower and outmaneuver the kingdom of Satan when the kingdom of God is accessed through His people. The two kingdoms are not equal in their power, and the kingdom of darkness cannot stand against the kingdom of God. Jesus said, *"On this rock* [the revelation from God about who Jesus is] *I will build my church, and the gates of Hades* **will not overcome it.** *I will give you the keys of the kingdom of heaven* [a euphemism for authority, like the keys to the city]*"* (Matthew 16:18–19; bold added).

So the kingdom did not come into existence when Jesus began His ministry on earth, but it did become newly available on the earth. The kingdom that had always been in existence in the heavenly realms became directly active in the circumstances of earth through the life of Jesus. *"But if I drive out demons by the Spirit of God, then the kingdom of God has come upon you"* (Matthew 12:28).

In this study of the parables of Rabbi Jesus, the focus will be primarily the present kingdom. Jesus's parables were to teach how to recognize the kingdom, how the kingdom operates, and how to live in the kingdom now.

Explain how the kingdom of God is eternal and has always been.

_____

_____

_____

_____

Explain how the kingdom of God is future and yet to be.

_____

_____

_____

_____

Explain how the kingdom of God is present-tense reality.

_____

_____

_____

_____

How would you fill in the following blank to define when the kingdom of God is in the present?

When the _____ **of God is in effect.**

The kingdom of God that Jesus taught and preached about is the rule and reign of God taking direct effect and being presently operative in the circumstances of earth. Jesus taught His disciples to pray, *"Your kingdom come, your will be done on earth as it is in heaven"* (Matthew 6:10). This is all one petition. A common literary device of Hebrew writing was to put two phrases side by side, saying the same thought in different words. The two thoughts elaborated on one another. *"Your kingdom come"* and *"your will be done"* are two ways of saying the same thing.

The verb tenses express urgency and immediacy: Right now—right this minute—Your rule and reign and authority and power must take effect in this circumstance; Your specific, intervening, good and perfect will must now be done, right here, right now. This is not a form of commanding God, but rather of agreeing with Him about the urgency and the importance of having His kingdom ruling at every moment and in every circumstance.

Kingdom Heralders and Citizens

The nation of Israel longed for the Messiah to appear. The Messiah's appearance was to be heralded by a return of Elijah. Elijah was to appear and prepare the people for the Messiah. Jesus said that John the Baptizer was the Elijah, the prophet they had been awaiting.

> *"But what did you go out to see? A prophet? Yes, I tell you, and more than a prophet. This is the one about whom it is written:*
>
> *"'I will send my messenger ahead of you,*
> *who will prepare your way before you.'"*
> —Luke 7:26–27

Jesus said John the Baptizer was the spirit of Elijah come in flesh. Of the prophets, Elijah was held in highest regard. At Jesus's transfiguration, Moses appeared to represent the Law, and Elijah appeared to represent the prophets. He was the superstar of prophets. Yet anyone who is a citizen of the kingdom is greater than John or Elijah. Jesus said:

> *"I tell you, among those born of women there is no one greater than John; yet the one who is least in the kingdom of God is greater than he."*
> —Luke 7:28

On a different occasion, Jesus emphasized this point, speaking of the kingdom: *"Blessed are your eyes because they see, and your ears because they hear. For I tell you the truth, many prophets and righteous men longed to see what you see but did not see it, and to hear what you hear but did not hear it"* (Matthew 13:16–17).

Here is what Jesus was saying to His audience: "You are more blessed than Moses or Elijah or David or any prophet or king or priest who ever lived. You have available to you what they could only long for. And even though John, the reembodiment of the spirit of Elijah, is the greatest man ever born of woman, you are greater still. You are born of God."

He said that up until the time of John the Baptizer, the kingdom was administered on the earth through the Law and the Prophets.

In other words, heaven entered earth through the Holy Scriptures and the words of the prophets, who were known as the Lord's mouthpieces. The direct action of God upon mankind was administered through the very limited conduits of the Law and the Prophets.

But now, the kingdom has fully come in the person of Jesus—God living and active among His people, clothed in flesh like theirs, making His home among them.

> *"The Law and the Prophets were proclaimed until John. Since that time, the good news of the kingdom of God is being preached, and everyone is forcing his way into it."*
> —Luke 16:16

> *In the past God spoke to our forefathers through the prophets at many times and in various ways, but in these last days he has spoken to us by his Son.*
> —Hebrews 1:1–2

Forceful Advancement of the Kingdom

The kingdom has come and everyone is welcome. The kingdom has come and even those of lowest status in the earth are great and esteemed in the kingdom. As the kingdom is revealed, there is a stampede to get in because it is the deepest longing in the hearts of men.

> *"From the days of John the Baptist until now, the kingdom of heaven has been forcefully advancing, and forceful men lay hold of it. For all the Prophets and the Law prophesied until John. And if you are willing to accept it, he is the Elijah who was to come. He who has ears, let him hear."*
> —Matthew 11:12–15

According to Lois Tverberg and Bruce Okkema, in their book, *Listening to the Language of the Bible*, "The word for 'violence,' *biazo* in Greek, also can mean 'forceful,' 'bursting out,' or even 'explosive,' which in Hebrew is *poretz*. Translators now believe that instead of the kingdom being victim of violence, Jesus was describing the explosive force of the kingdom!"

The references to *"forcefully advancing"* and *"forceful men lay hold of it"* set up a picture in the minds of the hearers. Jesus was speaking phrases and imagery familiar to His listeners. For those who first heard Him, these words called to mind the words of Micah:

> *"I will surely gather all of you, O Jacob;*
> > *I will surely bring together the remnant of Israel.*
> *I will bring them together like sheep in a pen,*
> > *like a flock in its pasture;*
> > *the place will throng with people.*
> *One who breaks open [haporetz] the way will go up before them;*
> > *they will break through [poretz] the gate and go out.*
> *Their king will pass through before them,*
> > *the LORD at their head."*
> —Micah 2:12–13

At night, a shepherd would shut up his sheep in a pen made with boulders. By morning, the sheep were hungry and restless and eager to get out into the fields. The shepherd would come and forcefully remove a boulder, making a way. It would have been a large boulder that he would have been required to move, and it would take much force to move it. Then the sheep, eager to get out to the fields, would come forcefully through the opening—a stampede brought on by eagerness, anticipation, and longing.

From the days of John the Baptizer, Jesus began and continued preaching the kingdom of heaven, forcefully pulling away the stone and opening the way. Those who had been kept by the Law and the Prophets, eagerly anticipating the coming kingdom, were rushing, stampeding into the freedom and abundance that the kingdom offers.

Jesus, the Door

Jesus is the Door—the opening—through which the kingdom of heaven has come into direct and immediate contact with the circumstances of earth. In Jesus, heaven and earth have a meeting place.

My son Brantley wrote beautifully about this very aspect of Jesus—His bringing heaven into earth and earth into heaven.

He is the leaven in the bread of our humanity, becoming inseparable from us and, having worked His way through the whole lump, causes us to be raised up to the divine. Indeed, despised and forsaken on the cross, His mortal breath is exhaled and releases that which was condemned from all condemnation. For those who could not possibly breathe the Godhead, He comes in a form as temporal as a breath and breathes His eternity into us. Christ's assuming of humanity is the analogy for our own partaking of His divine nature. Our ascension mirrors His condescension.

—Brantley Dean

See how the kingdom comes? Jesus infects us with Himself. He leavens us with Himself. He *does for us* and then *becomes in us* that which we cannot do or become. He brings heaven into earth and earth into heaven.

How do you understand the kingdom of God as it is present right now?

_____

_____

_____

_____

How is Jesus the Door to the kingdom?

_____

_____

_____

_____

Now Rabbi Jesus will begin to teach us how to live in the kingdom minute by minute, day by day. He will reframe our reality until the kingdom is in focus. Take His yoke upon you. Learn from Him.

DAY 5

Jesus spoke all these things to the crowd in parables; he did not say anything to them without using a parable. So was fulfilled what was spoken through the prophet:

> *"I will open my mouth in parables,*
> *I will utter things hidden since the creation of the world."*

—Matthew 13:34–35

Parables, a Method of Teaching

The use of parables for teaching was the most common of the rabbinical teaching methods. Talmud is filled with parables illustrating the fine points of Torah interpretation. Many of Jesus's parables played off familiar parabolic themes from Talmud.

The Hebrew word *masal,* translated by the Greek word *parabole,* translates into the English as "parable." A parable, from a rabbi's point of view, is an illustrative story that compares or contrasts an earthly reality with a spiritual truth. It is also a wise saying, a play on words, or even a rhythmic word grouping, a poem, a riddle, or an irony. By speaking truth in a masal, the rabbi would make the concept memorable. Since all of learning was accomplished by memorization, the more memorable a rabbi could make his presentation, the easier it would be for his disciples to learn it.

In this study, we will focus on the stories that Jesus told, but will supplement them with other forms of His masal, His parables.

To be a great teacher in Jesus's day and culture, which Jesus was, took intelligence, imagination, creativity, wisdom, and spontaneity. During the many months of study I have done in preparation for writing this Bible study, I have become captivated by Jesus's wit and sparkle. Crowds in the thousands sat spellbound, listening to Him teach. People were so captivated by Him, they forgot to eat (Mark 8:1–3). There were many gifted rabbis they could have listened to, but Jesus spoke as no man had ever spoken before.

In many cases, Jesus's parables seemed to be made up on the spur of the moment. The particular question and the setting and the immediate circumstance were the arena for His stories. Jesus was quick. He was charismatic and likeable. He was insightful and could see right to the heart of the questioner. He definitely did not intone long sermons, long faced and monotone. He engaged His audience. He was witty and clever. He was compelling.

Rabbinical teaching was done in basically three forms, and Jesus incorporated all three forms in His teaching.

- *Halakah*—legal interpretations; the details of how to keep the Law
- *Midrash*—exposition of the Holy Scriptures; we call it Bible study
- *Haggadah*—stories and other rhetorical devices meant to teach a deeper truth

Brad H. Young, in his book *The Parables*, teaches us that the goal of *haggadah*—parables, for example—is to teach God's way among His people and to help them understand the divine ways. According to *Sifre Devarim*, as edited by Louis Finkelstein, the rabbis teach, "If your desire is to know Him who spoke and the world came into being, then study Haggadah and you will know Him who spoke the world into being and you will cleave to His ways." Haggadah could reach people of all levels, from the learned scholar to the unschooled. Brad Young says that the goal of haggadah is to reach the heart through the imagination.

Parables, the Language of God

The Scripture, from beginning to end, is full of parables. God always speaks in parables. Everything He does, everything He creates, everything He says is telling a story. He has, from the beginning, woven a story that portrays for us the greatest story. The reality of redemption is far beyond our ability to comprehend, except that the Great Rabbi, the Eternal Rabbi, has taught us through stories designed to reach our hearts through our imagination.

The earth is a story. The Creation is a parable. Some of you who have read other books of mine or worked through my other Bible studies will see that I am about to return to a favorite theme. The earth is a picture—detailed and ingenious, the height of creativity. It is a parable of God. His invisible qualities and divine nature have been etched in clay. His transcendent glory has been cast in earthly forms (Romans 1:20).

> The entire moral and visible world, with its kings and its subjects, its sun and its moon, its sleeping and its waking, and all its variety of operations, is one mighty parable.... Christ moved in the midst of what seemed to the eye of sense an old and worn-out world, and it became new at his touch; for it told to man the inmost secrets of his being, and he found that of these two worlds, without him, and within, each threw a light and glory on the other.... Obnoxious to change, tainted with decay, all earthly things are weak and temporary, when they undertake to set forth things strong and eternal. They break down under the weight that is laid upon them.
>
> —R. C. Trench, *Notes on the Parables of Our Lord*

As R. C. Trench says, the earthly forms are not quite the full expression of the eternal. The earthly forms are tainted with decay, weak, and temporary. The illustration breaks down at some point along the way. But it provides for us the shadow and the outline from which we might envision the reality.

The Incarnation is a parable. The eternal Word took on flesh so that He could be the Word, act the Word, among His people. Also in *Notes on the Parables of Our Lord,* Trench says, "He gave no doctrine in an abstract form, no skeleton of truth, but clothed them all, as it were, in flesh and blood." He was God in a form that made Him accessible. The Eternal One walked the earth, knowable and touchable.

> *That which was from the beginning, which we have heard, which we have seen with our eyes, which we have looked at and our hands have touched—this we proclaim concerning the Word of life. The life appeared; we have seen it and testify to it, and we proclaim to you the eternal life, which was with the Father and has appeared to us. We proclaim to you what we have seen and heard.*
> —1 John 1:1–3

When I say the Incarnation is a parable, I don't mean that it is not historically and literally true. I mean that our Great Rabbi, our Eternal Father, condescended to our finite world and fit His infinite story of love and redemption into a narrative so that we could grasp at least the edges of His ways. *"Indeed these are the mere edges of His ways, And how small a whisper we hear of Him! But the thunder of His power who can understand?"* (Job 26:14 NKJV).

Every step that Jesus took on Planet Earth, the spiritual realm was shouting: "This is what God is like!" As He healed and taught and touched and laughed and loved, "This is what God is like!" As He hung broken on the cross, "This is what God is like!" When He rose from the grave and triumphed over death, "This is what God is like!"

> *The Son is the radiance of God's glory and the exact representation of his being.*
> —Hebrews 1:3

Parables, Parables, and More Parables

The tabernacle is a parable of the One who would someday dwell in His people. The sacrificial system is a parable of the redemption. Canaan is a parable of the kingdom of God. The true stories of God's dealing with

His people are also parables. *"These things happened to them as examples and were written down as warnings for us, on whom the fulfillment of the ages has come"* (1 Corinthians 10:11).

God acts in our lives in parables. Experiences we have become parables. Things we observe are the stuff of parables. I wear shoes with very high heels and very pointy toes because they are pretty. When the end of the day comes, and I remove the painful shoes and compare the shape of my foot with the shape of that shoe, I am reminded of how foolish it is to try to squeeze myself into a mold that doesn't fit me, all for the sake of appearance. I lose my way in a strange city and have to stop and ask a stranger for directions. The stranger turns out to be on staff at the church I'm trying to find and is, at this very time, on his way to that church. I'm reminded that God never loses me. We live in parables.

Eternal truth cast in earthly forms—that is God's way. It has always been God's way. God speaks in parables.

Be observant for parables in your life this week. Write out at least one.

_____

_____

_____

_____

_____

_____

_____

_____

As we begin to learn from Rabbi Jesus through His parables, we will look at three things: context, text, and subtext.

- *Context:* What was the setting in which this parable was spoken? How did the historical and cultural context define the characters or their actions?
- *Text:* What is the story?
- *Subtext:* What secret was Jesus sharing? What can we learn about the kingdom of God from this parable?

Then, bringing what we learned, we will come back to this pivotal question: Based on what Jesus disclosed about the kingdom, what does it mean to pray, as we are taught in the Lord's prayer, *"Your kingdom come, your will be done, on earth as it is in heaven"* (Matthew 6:10)?

WEEK ONE

SEEK
THE
KINGDOM

DAY 1

We begin this week to look at the stories Jesus told to illustrate who God is and how the kingdom of God operates. In looking at these stories and allowing Jesus to be our teacher, we won't try to press every detail into service. Some of the details were included to add texture to the story. A parable is not an allegory. In an allegory, each detail stands concretely for something or someone. In a parable, one central message is presented and some of the details are simply framework.

Parables were abundant in rabbinical teaching. The Talmud contains numerous parables. Jesus's parables borrowed from parables of His day. Most people knew the most popular parables, so when Jesus started a parable that sounded much like one they knew, His audience thought they knew what was coming. Jesus, a masterful storyteller, would have them following along, nodding their heads right in sync with Him. Then He would suddenly throw in a completely unexpected twist. When telling His parable, He would go completely off script and in a direction none of His listeners had anticipated.

He told some of His parables to the crowds as He taught them, but others, He told only to His inner-circle disciples.

Costs and Rewards of Discipleship

The parables we will look at this week are stories that teach us how to seek and find the kingdom. Those who enter the kingdom become disciples of the King. These parables introduce us to the costs and the rewards of discipleship.

> *"The kingdom of heaven is like treasure hidden in a field. When a man found it, he hid it again, and then in his joy went and sold all he had and bought that field.*
>
> *"Again, the kingdom of heaven is like a merchant looking for fine pearls. When he found one of great value, he went away and sold everything he had and bought it."*
> —Matthew 13:44–46

These twin parables Jesus told to His inner circle. They had already moved to a deeper level of commitment to Jesus than the crowds that came and went. As His disciples, they had left family, home, and businesses to learn from Him day and night. It was both exhilarating and demanding. The life of a disciple was no easy life.

Hidden Treasure

The first parable implies a man stumbled across something of great value hidden in a field. The description is vague. It certainly could have been something valuable that someone had buried for safekeeping, a common practice of the time; I think, though, that it was assumed that the treasure was something that occupied the whole field. In order to possess the treasure, one would have to possess the field. I think Jesus's audience more likely understood the treasure to be something like a gold mine or a silver mine, with veins of the treasure running all through the field.

As I try to hear this story through the ears of His contemporaries, several things are suggested in the context. His audience would have heard all these things without Jesus having to spell them out.

The man evidently was not scrupulously honest. The hearer wouldn't automatically think that he had integrity because he didn't just take the treasure, but instead went to buy the field. After all, apparently he kept the treasure a secret and did not disclose it to the seller.

Also, by Jewish law, he sinned by not disclosing that which was lost. The treasure he found would not legally belong to him, but to the one who had misplaced it. Buying the field would not give him legal ownership of the treasure. Talmud was very detailed about how long one had to try to find the owner of a lost item before the finder could take possession of it legally. This buyer did not try to find the owner at all.

The last point makes me think that the field itself embodied the treasure—that the treasure was hidden in and inseparable from the field. It was not a treasure that could be dug up and carried off. It had to be mined and extracted.

Look at the following passages and underline or highlight to what the Word of God compares treasure:

My son, if you accept my words
    and store up my commands within you,
turning your ear to wisdom
    and applying your heart to understanding,
and if you call out for insight
    and cry aloud for understanding,
and if you look for it as for silver
    and search for it as for hidden treasure,
then you will understand the fear of the LORD
    and find the knowledge of God.
For the LORD gives wisdom,
    and from his mouth come knowledge and understanding.
—**Proverbs 2:1–6**

Blessed is the man who finds wisdom,
    the man who gains understanding,
for she is more profitable than silver
    and yields better returns than gold.
She is more precious than rubies;
    nothing you desire can compare with her.
—**Proverbs 3:13–15**

"I, wisdom, dwell together with prudence;
    I possess knowledge and discretion....
With me are riches and honor,
    enduring wealth and prosperity.

My fruit is better than fine gold;
  what I yield surpasses choice silver.
I walk in the way of righteousness,
  along the paths of justice,
bestowing wealth on those who love me
  and making their treasuries full."
—**Proverbs 8:12, 18–21**

What is the treasure?

Many sayings of the rabbis, as do the Holy Scriptures, equate wisdom and knowledge with treasure.

The belief of the Jewish people was that, on Mount Sinai, God revealed all truth to Moses. Moses wrote it down in the Torah—the first five books of the Bible. The words of the Torah contained all truth, but much of the truth was hidden. The role of sages and rabbis was to extract the hidden truths. They mined wisdom from every phrase and every word. The body of truth extracted from Torah was the Talmud, the oral law.

You can see how Jesus's audience would have made many associations that we might miss. Knowledge of Torah and wisdom from above were often referred to as treasure. Much of that treasure was hidden from sight and could not be observed on the surface. It would not yield itself simply by digging a hole and grabbing hold of it. The treasure had to be mined, carefully and skillfully. The veins of treasure ran throughout the whole Torah, rather than being plopped into one hole, one place. Seekers, such as those in Jesus's audience, were always on the lookout for new veins of treasure not yet discovered.

In this parable Jesus shared, the twist came when the man rushed out immediately and sold everything he owned and invested all in one field. This field was worth everything to him. Nothing else compared to possessing this field. Everything the man had owned, valued, and worked for previously seemed worthless. All that mattered was possessing the treasure hidden in the field. The Apostle Paul understood this concept:

But whatever was to my profit I now consider loss for the sake of Christ. What is more, I consider everything a loss compared to the surpassing greatness of knowing Christ Jesus my Lord, for whose sake I have lost all things. I consider them rubbish, that I may gain Christ and be found in him, not having a righteousness of my own that comes from the law, but that which is through faith in Christ—the righteousness that comes from God and is by faith. I want to know Christ and the power of his resurrection and the fellowship of sharing in his sufferings, becoming like him in his death, and so, somehow, to attain to the resurrection from the dead.
—Philippians 3:7–11

Read these passages, and answer the question that follows:

My purpose is that they may be encouraged in heart and united in love, so that they may have the full riches of complete understanding, in order that they may know the mystery of God, namely, Christ, in whom are hidden all the treasures of wisdom and knowledge.
—Colossians 2:2–3

He will be the sure foundation for your times,
 a rich store of salvation and wisdom and knowledge;
  the fear of the LORD is the key to this treasure.
—Isaiah 33:6

For God, who said, "Let light shine out of darkness," made his light shine in our hearts to give us the light of the knowledge of the glory of God in the face of Christ.
 But we have this treasure in jars of clay to show that this all-surpassing power is from God and not from us.
—2 Corinthians 4:6–7

WEEK TWO

Where is the real treasure hidden?

_____

_____

_____

The kingdom is present in Jesus. Only in Him will the riches of the kingdom be found. He is the Eternal Torah made flesh, the Living Torah. Everything mankind desires is to be found in Him.

The kingdom does not have visitors—it has subjects. To enter the kingdom of God, you have to leave behind everything else. The kingdom will cost you everything.

A woman interviewed on a news show said she bought an abstract painting from a junk store in California for $5. Ten years after her purchase, she discovered that the "junk" she purchased was likely an original Jackson Pollock painting and could be worth more than $10 million.

Let's project our imaginations into the future and suppose that the woman has been paid $10 million for the painting that cost her $5. Let's imagine that she is sitting in the palatial mansion the money has afforded her and that she is dripping in jewels and draped in fine designer clothing, none of which she could have afforded previously. Imagine that I ask her, "What did that Jackson Pollock painting cost you?" How do you think she would answer that question? I think she would say, "Cost me? It cost me nothing. It gained me $10 million and afforded me everything I own."

When the profit far outweighs the investment, we call it gain. The initial cost is swallowed up in the benefit it obtains, resulting in a show of profit on the balance sheet.

Isn't that what Paul was saying in Philippians 3:7–11? He said that he gave up everything he valued because when he compared it to _"the surpassing greatness of knowing Christ Jesus [his] Lord,"_ everything he valued was rubbish. Nothing. Less than nothing. The worth of everything he valued was swallowed up in the surpassing greatness of knowing Christ. If we could ask Paul, "What did radical discipleship cost you?" I think Paul would answer, "Cost me? It cost me nothing and gained me everything."

Pearl of Great Value

The second of these twin parables goes like this: *"Again, the kingdom of heaven is like a merchant looking for fine pearls. When he found one of great value, he went away and sold everything he had and bought it"* (Matthew 13:45–46).

Jesus told the two parables as one. "Again" is the translation of a conjunction Jesus used that tied the two together into one. This is a very common rabbinical device—saying basically the same thing two different ways, adding depth to the picture.

In this second parable, the person who found the treasure was looking for that very treasure. He didn't just happen upon some unspecified treasure. He had spent his career searching for fine pearls. He knew pearls. He had examined more pearls than he could count. He knew what to look for in a pearl.

After all that time, all his effort, all his investment, he found one pearl that he knew immediately was the one he had been looking for. In his mind's eye, he compared it with all the other pearls he had bought over the years, and they all fell short. None of them could come close. This pearl was worth all the others combined…and more. This pearl was worth everything he owned.

Like the man who stumbled across a treasure in a field by accident, this man immediately sold all he had and bought what he treasured—the one pearl. The pearl cost him everything.

Who do you think the merchant was? Who in Jesus's day had spent their lives searching out the treasures of Torah? Who among Jesus's peers had been hungrily seeking the one pearl that would satisfy their quest for wisdom?

With these twin parables, Jesus invited both the scholarly, learned leader and the unschooled peasant into the kingdom. The cost was the same for both: everything they had. The reward was the same for both: everything He has.

What is Rabbi Jesus saying to you? On what are you placing too much value? What is holding your heart other than Him?

Let Your Kingdom Come

Based on what God has taught you through the parables of the hidden treasure and the pearl of great value, what does it mean to pray, "Let Your kingdom come"?

DAY 2

Today we will examine a parable recorded by Luke, still looking at the theme of what it costs to possess the kingdom. Discipleship is not cheap, and Jesus wants to make sure that those who follow Him realize that His call is to a full-time vocation. Not every Christ follower earns his or her living in ministry, but every Christ follower is in full-time service to Him. Anyone who takes His yoke commits himself to a completely new way of living.

The Rich Fool

The parable to which we'll give our attention today is the parable of the rich fool. Luke sets the scene. Jesus is at the height of His popularity. In fact, as this story unfolds, Luke says, *"Meanwhile, when a crowd of many thousands had gathered, so that they were trampling on one another, Jesus began to speak first to his disciples"* (Luke 12:1). Among the crowd were those who were accepting and embracing His message, those who were curious about this phenomenon and considering His message, and those who were hostile to Him and hoping to catch Him in an error.

He began to speak to His inner circle of disciples, although the crowd was listening as well. He was teaching them on several subjects. (It is doubtful that Luke recorded every single word; he just gave an overview of the topics Jesus was addressing and some of His words. Luke was not present. He wrote his Gospel years after the events and used several sources for his research.) Considering the thousands in the crowd, and taking into account the custom of a rabbi's public teaching, this discourse probably went on for most of the day.

When a rabbi taught publicly, those listening were not expected to be quiet. Instead, they were expected to chime in with questions. It was not a quiet setting where students sat politely and took notes and looked up verses in their Bibles. They jostled to get closer. They called out questions. Life and commerce went on in the background.

In the middle of all this energy and chaos, someone from the crowd called out a legal question. This was not unusual because rabbis were the ones who interpreted the Torah into everyday life. They were often called on to decide a legal question.

Someone in the crowd said to him, "Teacher, tell my brother to divide the inheritance with me."

Jesus replied, "Man, who appointed me a judge or an arbiter between you?" Then he said to them, "Watch out! Be on your guard against all kinds of greed; a man's life does not consist in the abundance of his possessions."

And he told them this parable: "The ground of a certain rich man produced a good crop. He thought to himself, 'What shall I do? I have no place to store my crops.'

"Then he said, 'This is what I'll do. I will tear down my barns and build bigger ones, and there I will store all my grain and my goods. And I'll say to myself, "You have plenty of good things laid up for many years. Take life easy; eat, drink and be merry."'

"But God said to him, 'You fool! This very night your life will be demanded from you. Then who will get what you have prepared for yourself?'

"This is how it will be with anyone who stores up things for himself but is not rich toward God."
—Luke 12:13–21

The man asked Jesus to make his brother divide the inheritance with him. When the father in a Jewish household died, the majority of the estate went to the eldest son, who was then to divide the remainder among the others. We are not told or given any strong hints about the problem here. Jesus didn't ask for further details. He did not address the words of the man, but instead addressed the heart of the man.

Jesus was brilliant at using the teachable moment, and He didn't need an outline or any other tools. He had truth. He was the storehouse of wisdom; it was His native language. In response to the man's question, He changed direction and addressed the heart issue at hand.

The man might have had a legitimate legal issue. He might indeed have been treated unfairly by his brother. We don't know. Jesus made it clear that His mission was not to address legal issues, but to address kingdom issues.

He shared a parable about a man who was so caught up in accumulating and holding on to wealth for himself that he missed the kingdom. The character in this story was a man so successful and so wealthy that he had no room to store it all.

Read through the parable and highlight or underline all the personal first-person references (me, my, mine, I).

Who was the lodestar of this man's universe?

With whom did he discuss his dilemma?

In the whole story, do you see any other character with whom he had relationship?

What had his possessions become for him?

This rich man invested himself in the wrong things. In direct contrast to the characters in the twin parables of hidden treasure and pearl of great price, this man held tightly to all he owned. The rich fool did not realize that *"life is more than food, and the body more than clothes"* (Luke 12:23).

Let's get back to the man who asked Jesus the question that had to do with the distribution of his father's estate—that which the father had worked all his life to amass. I wonder if Jesus might have known the questioner. The man didn't seem to think he needed to give Jesus any details. He asked the question as if Jesus knew the details. Jesus responded as if He knew the details. He read into the question many assumptions. Possibly, Jesus could just tell by the tone of the question, but I think He knew the man and knew the family. I think He knew the father who had died and left his estate, and apparently his greedy inclinations, to his sons. I think the parable described the father, and it described where the son was headed as he focused on the material wealth due him at the expense of the relationship with his brother. Not only did the man forfeit his relationships for his possessions, he also left behind sons who were about to do the same thing. They had inherited not just his possessions; they had inherited his priorities.

Focus, Not Fear

Does this parable speak only to those who have great wealth? No, it is not a story about wealth. It is a story about *focus.* Every one of us has something that, if we're not careful, could burrow into our hearts and crowd out the kingdom. Even those who are not rich can get their focus on material things to the exclusion of the kingdom. Jesus followed this parable with an extension of the point of the parable.

> *Then Jesus said to his disciples:* "**Therefore** *I tell you, do not worry about your life, what you will eat; or about your body, what you will wear. Life is more than food, and the body more than clothes. Consider the ravens: They do not sow or reap, they have no storeroom or barn; yet God feeds them. And how much more valuable you are than birds! Who of you by worrying can add a single hour to his life? Since you cannot do this very little thing, why do you worry about the rest?*
>
> *"Consider how the lilies grow. They do not labor or spin. Yet I tell you, not even Solomon in all his splendor was dressed like one of these. If that is how God clothes the grass of the field, which is here today, and tomorrow is thrown into the fire, how much more will he clothe you, O you of little faith! And do not set your heart on what you will eat or drink; do not worry about it. For the pagan world runs after all such things, and your Father knows that you need them. But seek his kingdom, and these things will be given to you as well.*
>
> *"Do not be afraid, little flock, for your Father has been pleased to give you the kingdom. Sell your possessions and give to the poor. Provide purses for yourselves that will not wear out, a treasure in heaven that will not be exhausted, where no thief comes near and no moth destroys. For where your treasure is, there your heart will be also."*
>
> —Luke 12:22–34; bold added

The word *therefore* ties this teaching to what has come before. This is all one teaching about *focus.* If you are rich, you could be in danger of getting your heart entangled with your possessions. If you are not rich, you could be in danger of focusing on your need and your anxiety.

Then Jesus presented another parable-style teaching. He pointed to earth as a visual to explain how God acts with His people. You can imagine the scene. Jesus, responding to the moment, looked around and, in the sky, saw a raven. "Look at the ravens," He said, pointing. *"They do not sow or reap, they have no storeroom or barn; yet God feeds them."* (Do you see how He referred back to the parable of the rich fool whose concern was the size of his barns?) Then He looked around and saw one of the many lilies that grew in the crevices of the pathways, with no evidence of water or soil; they just stuck their heads up through the dry, dusty, cracked earth. Here and there, lilies grew in the most unlikely environment. "Look at that lily," Jesus said, pointing. *"Consider how the lilies grow. They do not labor or spin. Yet I tell you, not even Solomon in all his splendor was dressed like one of these."*

Then He made a typical rabbinical argument. The form is called "from lesser to greater." He proved a point beyond any doubt, and then extrapolated that principle to something bigger. *"If that is how God clothes the grass of the field, which is here today, and tomorrow is thrown into the fire, how much more will he clothe you, O you of little faith!"*

Then He made the point He had been illustrating: *"And do not set your heart on what you will eat or drink; do not worry about it. For the pagan world runs after all such things, and your Father knows that you need them. But seek his kingdom, and these things will be given to you as well."* Instead of worrying about where you will store your wealth or worrying about how you will meet your needs, seek the kingdom.

Now watch this point. The kingdom is invisible, yet those who have entered the kingdom will see its effects in the material realm. Jesus tells His disciples that when they seek the kingdom, all the things they need will be added to them as well. The kingdom is operating when the will of God is directly in effect in a situation. The kingdom is not relegated to the spiritual realm. It invades the circumstances of earth.

What threatens to distract you from the kingdom?

_____

_____

_____

_____

How do those distractions sneak in, and what usually alerts you to their presence?

_____

_____

_____

_____

Treasures in Heaven

Matthew put this teaching about your treasures in a grouping, not really putting it in a setting. He included other parabolic sayings around it. Find Matthew 6:19–34 in your Bible and note the surrounding text.

> *"Do not store up for yourselves treasures on earth, where moth and rust destroy, and where thieves break in and steal. But store up for yourselves treasures in heaven, where moth and rust do not destroy, and where thieves do not break in and steal. For where your treasure is, there your heart will be also.*
>
> *"The eye is the lamp of the body. If your eyes are good, your whole body will be full of light. But if your eyes are bad, your whole body will be full of darkness. If then the light within you is darkness, how great is that darkness!*
>
> *"No one can serve two masters. Either he will hate the one and love the other, or he will be devoted to the one and despise the other. You cannot serve both God and Money.*

"Therefore I tell you, do not worry about your life, what you will eat or drink; or about your body, what you will wear. Is not life more important than food, and the body more important than clothes? Look at the birds of the air; they do not sow or reap or store away in barns, and yet your heavenly Father feeds them. Are you not much more valuable than they? Who of you by worrying can add a single hour to his life?

"And why do you worry about clothes? See how the lilies of the field grow. They do not labor or spin. Yet I tell you that not even Solomon in all his splendor was dressed like one of these. If that is how God clothes the grass of the field, which is here today and tomorrow is thrown into the fire, will he not much more clothe you, O you of little faith? So do not worry, saying, 'What shall we eat?' or 'What shall we drink?' or 'What shall we wear?' For the pagans run after all these things, and your heavenly Father knows that you need them. But seek first his kingdom and his righteousness, and all these things will be given to you as well. Therefore do not worry about tomorrow, for tomorrow will worry about itself. Each day has enough trouble of its own."
—Matthew 6:19–34

Rabbi Jesus used His skill at *masal* (saying truths in memorable ways) to make this important teaching about the kingdom easy to remember. In both the Luke and Matthew accounts, this teaching includes the point that those who are in the kingdom can be generous to those around them because God will take care of all their needs. Kingdom-focused living frees you from anxiety about temporal things so you can express the kingdom into the circumstances of earth.

In this passage from Matthew, Jesus is quoted as using a Hebrew idiom—"good eye" and "bad eye." To have a "good eye" means to be generous; to have a "bad eye" means to be stingy.

Read again through Luke's version (12:22–34) of Jesus's teaching on kingdom-focused living, and see what it says. Having no fear of lack, you can let go of material possessions and be wildly and extravagantly generous.

Jesus is not saying that it is wrong to have wealth if you come by it honestly and honorably. But you must guard against letting your possessions own your heart. You must guard against letting your possessions hold the place the kingdom should occupy. Don't put your faith in your possessions. The best way to guard against that is to be generous. Hold them loosely.

The kingdom will cost you everything.

Go through Matthew 6:19–34 and restate each thought in your own words, as if you were saying it to someone right now.

LET YOUR KINGDOM COME

Based on what God has taught you so far through the parable of the rich fool, what does it mean to pray, "Let Your kingdom come"?

DAY 3

One Sabbath, Jesus was the guest of a prominent Pharisee, and by that time, we read in Luke 14, He was being watched closely. It was in the last weeks before the Crucifixion, and His enemies were closing in. They were waiting for a misstep so they could bring charges against Him. Instead of backing off, Jesus was being increasingly bold, pointed, and confrontational in His teaching.

Jesus healed a man on that Sabbath—a definite taboo. And, while healing the man, He challenged the Pharisees and the experts in the Law about it, leaving them defenseless. Then at the banquet, He voiced an observation about how the guests vied for the best seats and jostled to put themselves in places of honor. He was bold, pointed, confrontational.

Read Luke 14:1–11 to picture the setting of this parable. Put yourself in the setting. What must the atmosphere have been like? What were the undercurrents? What were people whispering to one another?

Jesus knew He was being watched. He knew that Herod was watching for an opportunity to kill Him (Luke 13:31). He knew His enemies among the

Jewish elite were hoping to trap Him in an argument either to discredit Him with the crowds or to bring charges against Him. Yet He was deliberately confrontational. Imagine the scene as He was about to heal the man with dropsy. Look at the verses again that describe that scene.

> *One Sabbath, when Jesus went to eat in the house of a prominent Pharisee, he was being carefully watched. There in front of him was a man suffering from dropsy. Jesus asked the Pharisees and experts in the law, "Is it lawful to heal on the Sabbath or not?" But they remained silent. So taking hold of the man, he healed him and sent him away.*
>
> *Then he asked them, "If one of you has a son or an ox that falls into a well on the Sabbath day, will you not immediately pull him out?" And they had nothing to say.*
> —Luke 14:1–6

The phrase *"when Jesus went to eat"* is better translated *"as Jesus was going to eat."* The story was first told in Hebrew, then translated into Greek, then into English. Hebrew verb tenses are not as clear-cut as either Greek or English, so sometimes the tenses get lost in translation. In the Matthew and Mark accounts of the story, Jesus was at the synagogue when He healed the man. This makes sense, because those who were physically handicapped would ask alms (beg) outside the temple or synagogue. Giving alms was considered one of the highest expressions of righteousness. When a person gave alms at the temple or the synagogue, he could be seen and admired. It was a good place for beggars to find a steady stream of alms givers. Read the other accounts in Mark 3:1–5 and Matthew 12:9–13.

It was understood that Jesus was going to the house of a prominent Pharisee—a man who was scrupulous about the Law. This man had invited Jesus to eat at his house for only one reason: to catch Him in a mistake. On the way, right in front of Jesus, was a man with dropsy. This disease caused tremors and weakness in the hand. The text seems to indicate that the man did not ask for healing. Probably he asked Jesus for alms, as he was asking all the passersby for alms. Probably others had given alms, dropping their coins from high so they would make a loud sound when they landed and other persons would notice their righteousness.

Jesus's antagonists saw Him stop and take notice of this man. Their excitement mounted as they anticipated what was to come. Jesus was going to flout the law of the Sabbath, right there in front of everyone; it was the very moment they had been waiting for.

SECRETS JESUS SHARED

Jesus turned to them. I want you to imagine Jesus with a twinkle in His eye and a wry smile on His face. He got it. He knew what they were hoping for. "Hey, guys!" Familiar. Casual. "So, tell Me. Are we allowed to heal on the Sabbath? What do you think?"

Wouldn't you think they would jump right in? They had the law on their side. The people were watching. Among their ranks, there was no disagreement about this issue. It was cut and dried, black and white.

Yet they didn't say a word. I'm imagining their inner dialogue: "That question must have a catch. That's too easy. We've fallen into this trap before. We've seen His debating style. He lulls us with an obvious question, then springs His trap and catches us in an inconsistency. He leaves us looking foolish before the crowds. We'd better just be quiet. Let Him hang Himself."

Maybe Jesus waited a beat or two, giving them a chance to pounce. No objections? Jesus healed the man and sent him on his way. Then He turned to the Pharisees. Even though they weren't bold enough to say it out loud, He knew their opinion. "So, let's imagine that you have...oh, let's say, a son...or even an ox,...you know, something that you value. And it falls into a ditch on the Sabbath. Wouldn't you immediately pull it out? Wouldn't you rescue it?" Jesus left them speechless.

Location, Location, Location

That's the setting for this parable. They got to the house, and Jesus was watching the guests as they maneuvered their way into the most strategic positions. They wanted to be sure that their seat adequately announced their position.

Then came the parable of the great banquet:

Then Jesus said to his host, "When you give a luncheon or dinner, do not invite your friends, your brothers or relatives, or your rich neighbors; if you do, they may invite you back and so you will be repaid. But when you give a banquet, invite the poor, the crippled, the lame, the blind, and you will be blessed. Although they cannot repay you, you will be repaid at the resurrection of the righteous."

When one of those at the table with him heard this, he said to Jesus, "Blessed is the man who will eat at the feast in the kingdom of God."

Jesus replied: "A certain man was preparing a great banquet and invited many guests. At the time of the banquet he sent his servant to tell those who had been invited, 'Come, for everything is now ready.'

"But they all alike began to make excuses. The first said, 'I have just bought a field, and I must go and see it. Please excuse me.'

"Another said, 'I have just bought five yoke of oxen, and I'm on my way to try them out. Please excuse me.'

"Still another said, 'I just got married, so I can't come.'

"The servant came back and reported this to his master. Then the owner of the house became angry and ordered his servant, 'Go out quickly into the streets and alleys of the town and bring in the poor, the crippled, the blind and the lame.'

"'Sir,' the servant said, 'what you ordered has been done, but there is still room.'

"Then the master told his servant, 'Go out to the roads and country lanes and make them come in, so that my house will be full. I tell you, not one of those men who were invited will get a taste of my banquet.'"
—Luke 14:12–24

First, Jesus admonished His host. This might seem very rude to us, but really, in that day, it was not uncommon for one rabbi to challenge another or for a rabbi to confront someone. Then a lively debate—one in which everyone participated—would usually ensue. You see that scene often in Jesus's life. Many times, His teaching was in response to a challenge or to a question called out from the crowd.

Jesus challenged His host to put on a banquet for which there would be no payoff for the host. Invite guests who could not return the favor. The status of one's guests at a meal was a measure of the status of the host. The status of the host was the measure of the status of the guests. Important people associated with important people. Even the ability to give a banquet was a status symbol. A peasant couldn't afford to feed his own family sometimes, let alone a number of guests.

In response to Jesus's challenge, someone voiced a much-used saying: *"Blessed is the man who will eat at the feast in the kingdom of God."* It was commonly accepted doctrine that the messianic age and the rule of the kingdom of God would be ushered in with a great banquet. It would prove who was really, really important when the guest list of that great banquet was revealed.

The Guest List

Rabbinic literature contains more than 5,000 parables. A banquet was a frequent setting for parables. As Jesus started this parable, with a great banquet as the setting, His audience was in familiar territory.

In that day, a man would send out his servants to issue invitations to the banquet and to receive the responses of his guests. He would tell them the day, but not the hour. The hour would depend on when everything was ready. At the hour, a second invitation went out as the servants went back to the guests who had accepted and said, "The hour has come." Guests were to be ready and dressed when the second invitation came. They would leave immediately and make their way to the banquet.

Jesus told a story of a man who prepared a grand banquet—one with the best wine, choicest food, finest musicians, and most valuable tableware. His household had been in a frenzy of preparation for days. The sounds and the sights and the smells of the banquet being prepared spilled out into the streets. Everyone knew about the banquet.

The parable begins when the host sends out his second summons to tell the guests who had accepted his first invitation that the meal was ready. The hour had come. Each of the invitees in the story had already accepted the invitation.

The audience was right with Him—up to this point. They were along for the ride, comfortable in their well-worn ideas. Now for the twist: Jesus veered off course. The guests, who should be honored by the invitation and eagerly awaiting the summons, had forgotten all about it. All kinds of other things had diverted their attention. They had put their own business ahead of the banquet. They were distracted from the focus.

I think Jesus was being humorous with these excuses. All of them were silly and contrived. Who would buy land and have only one day to go look at it? Who would buy oxen without having tried them first? Who would plan a marriage between the time of the invitation and the dinner? Each excuse was sillier than the one before.

I think that was the point. Silly things got in the way of enjoying the banquet.

Of course, this was an insult to the host. It caused him to lose face before the whole village. And what would he do with all the food and wine? Many days of preparation had been put into this banquet.

The host sent his servant out to bring in the poor, the blind, and the lame. These were the outcasts in Jewish society. They were thought to be unclean and, thus, unable to attend the great banquet of the kingdom.

When those had been brought in, the servant said, *"There is still room."* Apparently grace, like nature, abhors a vacuum. The host told his servant to go out even further and invite with urgency those out in the countryside. The banquet was filled with people who had previously had no hope of sitting at a great banquet given by a great host.

WEEK TWO

Those who thought other things were more important missed the banquet altogether. Those who clung to their possessions and put their activities ahead of the invitation were, in the truest sense, poor, blind, and lame.

By clinging to what they owned, they lost everything.

What would you say is the kingdom secret in this parable? What is Rabbi Jesus whispering to you? Are you missing out on the banquet of the kingdom because something else has diverted your attention?

_____

_____

_____

_____

_____

LET YOUR KINGDOM COME

Based on what God has taught you so far through the parable of the great banquet, what does it mean to pray, "Let Your kingdom come"?

_____

_____

_____

_____

_____

DAY 4

Today we will look at a parable that Jesus used to teach further about the cost of the kingdom. The parable of the talents comes at the subject from a new direction, emphasizing investment and risk. It is one of the first parables you might have learned as a child, an often-told and much-discussed parable. Ask the Lord to reveal new truth to you as we study it.

Investing Your Talents

Matthew and Luke both provide a version of the parable of the talents (Matthew 25:14–30; Luke 19:12–27). Each Gospel tells it a little differently. I want to use Matthew's account as the primary account.

> *"Again, it will be like a man going on a journey, who called his servants and entrusted his property to them. To one he gave five talents of money, to another two talents, and to another one talent, each according to his ability. Then he went on his journey. The man who had received the five talents went at once and put his money to work and gained five more. So also, the one with the two talents gained two more. But the man who had received the one talent went off, dug a hole in the ground and hid his master's money.*
>
> *"After a long time the master of those servants returned and settled accounts with them. The man who had received the five talents brought the other five. 'Master,' he said, 'you entrusted me with five talents. See, I have gained five more.'*
>
> *"His master replied, 'Well done, good and faithful servant! You have been faithful with a few things; I will put you in charge of many things. Come and share your master's happiness!'*
>
> *"The man with the two talents also came. 'Master,' he said, 'you entrusted me with two talents; see, I have gained two more.'*
>
> *"His master replied, 'Well done, good and faithful servant! You have been faithful with a few things; I will put you in charge of many things. Come and share your master's happiness!'*
>
> *"Then the man who had received the one talent came. 'Master,' he said, 'I knew that you are a hard man, harvesting where you have not sown and gathering where you have not scattered seed. So*

I was afraid and went out and hid your talent in the ground. See, here is what belongs to you.'

"His master replied, 'You wicked, lazy servant! So you knew that I harvest where I have not sown and gather where I have not scattered seed? Well then, you should have put my money on deposit with the bankers, so that when I returned I would have received it back with interest.

"'Take the talent from him and give it to the one who has the ten talents. For everyone who has will be given more, and he will have an abundance. Whoever does not have, even what he has will be taken from him. And throw that worthless servant outside, into the darkness, where there will be weeping and gnashing of teeth.'"
—Matthew 25:14–30

Each Gospel specifies that Jesus told this parable because the people thought He was about to establish the kingdom physically. Clearly the primary purpose of this story was to show the people how the kingdom works in the now, the interim until the time He returns to establish the kingdom physically on the earth.

Jesus was telling a story. He was making His story entertaining and colorful. He created characters with personalities to act out the lesson. Don't try to attach each detail to a spiritual reality. God is not angry and vindictive. He certainly doesn't harvest where He has not sown or gather where He has not scattered seed. The master is a character and his harshness spawns urgency in his servants.

This parable had a direct cause: addressing the expectation of the immediate setting up of the earthly kingdom. But it illustrated a kingdom principle about how disciples of the King live.

The people were familiar with many parables about masters or kings who went away and left servants in charge. Once again, Jesus started down a familiar trail, then took an abrupt turn.

The money represents anything that God has entrusted us with: spiritual gifts, natural talents, faith, opportunities, time, relationships. No one could list every possibility. *"Every good and perfect gift is from above, coming down from the Father,"* according to James 1:17. This parable applies to the investment of anything that God has entrusted to us.

Investment means risk. Investment means that the growth is not immediate and requires patience and nerve. If we want to live in the fullness of the kingdom, we have to put ourselves at risk. The mistake that the servant with one talent made was that he feared losing what he had and, thus, lost the opportunity to gain more.

As you review this parable, do you think the first two servants had a different belief about the master than the third servant had?

_____

_____

What did the third servant believe about his master?

_____

_____

_____

What did the first two servants seem to believe about the master?

_____

_____

_____

What did the first two servants experience from the master?

_____

_____

_____

_____

What did the third servant experience from the master?

_____

_____

_____

_____

_____

Take a Risk

Jesus was talking to an audience who dealt with God and the Scripture with a great deal of fear. The scholars taught that there had to be a "hedge around Torah." In other words, they needed to develop a complicated series of laws that would keep a person from coming close to breaking the laws laid out in Torah. For example, the oral law that the name of God was not to be spoken or written was a hedge around Torah to prevent the possibility of breaking the commandment not to take the name of the Lord in vain. These laws became so detailed as to be ridiculous and took the daily joy out of the study of Torah and the worship of God. The people were so afraid of offending God that they missed out on experiencing the joy He had in them.

Jesus was saying, "Loosen up! Take a risk! God is not waiting for you to fail so He can punish you. He is waiting for you to succeed so He can celebrate with you."

God's people had been entrusted with His riches. He meant for them to invest them, not hoard them. The more you invest all that you have been given, the more it grows. The more you give, the more you get.

Notice that the third servant buried his money. That was the way people in Jesus's day kept their money safe.

One rabbinic parable describes a miser who sold everything he had, bought gold, and buried his gold in the ground. Every day he came to look at his gold. One night a thief stole his treasure. The next day when the miser came to look at his gold and discovered it was gone, he wailed and tore out his hair. A friend came along to ask him what was wrong. When the miser told him, the friend said, "Don't worry about it. Go get a stone and bury it in the ground and come look at it every day. It will do you as much good as your gold was doing you."

Jesus did not compromise on one single issue of the Law of God, but He knew the difference between the Law of God and the commands of men. He wasn't telling people to treat the Law lightly. He was trying to redefine their Master for them.

What secret has Jesus been whispering to you? Has He given you something that you are afraid of losing? How is He telling you to put it at risk and see it grow?

To fully experience the kingdom, you have to let go of fear. You have to be willing to hold everything loosely. You have to resist holding on to things in your grasp because the kingdom is worth everything.

LET YOUR KINGDOM COME

Based on what God has taught you through the parable of the talents, what does it mean to pray, "Let Your kingdom come"?

DAY 5

The call to the kingdom is a call to discipleship. It is a call to yoke yourself to Jesus. The salvation that Jesus has provided for us is full-spectrum salvation—body, soul, and spirit. When we answer the call to the kingdom, Jesus moves in and makes His home in us. Our *Rav Yeshua* teaches us day and night, not by being with us, but by being in us. We have the mind of Christ. He can make direct deposits from His mind to ours. He can transform the spirit of our minds. He can renew our thoughts. No other rabbi has ever had such direct access to the hearts and minds of His disciples. He speaks to us and He speaks through us. He impacts every level of our humanity. He calls for full surrender to Him.

Count the Cost and Go for It

So when He issues that invitation to the kingdom, He is inviting us not just to the outside edges but to the very heart of the kingdom. We don't have to sit on the sidelines. We can jump in with both feet. We can get in the deep end.

It's a big call. Jesus says we should think about the cost.

Large crowds were traveling with Jesus, and turning to them he said: "If anyone comes to me and does not hate his father and mother, his wife and children, his brothers and sisters—yes, even his own life—he cannot be my disciple. And anyone who does not carry his cross and follow me cannot be my disciple.

"Suppose one of you wants to build a tower. Will he not first sit down and estimate the cost to see if he has enough money to complete it? For if he lays the foundation and is not able to finish it, everyone who sees it will ridicule him, saying, 'This fellow began to build and was not able to finish.'

"Or suppose a king is about to go to war against another king. Will he not first sit down and consider whether he is able with ten thousand men to oppose the one coming against him with twenty thousand? If he is not able, he will send a delegation while the other is still a long way off and will ask for terms of peace. In the same way, any of you who does not give up everything he has cannot be my disciple."

—Luke 14:25–33

The message here is unambiguous. Look clearly at what it means to seek the kingdom and to be a disciple, and decide whether you want to cling to what you have or let go of it all and embrace the kingdom.

He is not saying that you need to sell your house and leave your family. He's just saying that everything has to be held in trust. You are not the owner; you are the trustee. All you have is at the King's disposal. All you have, you have been given to manage for the Owner. It is all His, and He can use it however He wants. The kingdom will cost you everything.

Look back over each day's material. Write out the main thing that God has said to you about your life this week.

_____

_____

_____

_____

_____

What is the biggest challenge you heard from Him this week?

_____

_____

_____

_____

_____

_____

What is the sweetest promise you heard from Him this week?

KINGDOM GROWTH

DAY 1

Rabbi Jesus put a particular emphasis on teaching His disciples about patience when it comes to experiencing the kingdom. In the kingdom, no value is placed on instant gratification. Process is as important as outcome. Even when you can't see the progress, you can trust that it is occurring.

This week we will examine parables about growth. They will give us insight into a kingdom principle. This growth principle works itself out in personal spiritual growth, in the growth of a ministry or action of kingdom service, and in the expansion of the kingdom as an entity. Kingdom growth is characterized by steady progress, although seemingly slow and often invisible for a time. Jesus knew that it was important for His disciples to understand the growth principle in the kingdom. Otherwise, they would be discouraged by what they saw or didn't see.

The Sower and the Four Soils

Jesus told a story about a sower who went out to sow. We'll focus on Mark's version of the parable:

Again Jesus began to teach by the lake. The crowd that gathered around him was so large that he got into a boat and sat in it out on the lake, while all the people were along the shore at the water's edge. He taught them many things by parables, and in his teaching said: "Listen! A farmer went out to sow his seed. As he was scattering the seed, some fell along the path, and the birds came and ate it up. Some fell on rocky places, where it did not have much soil. It sprang up quickly, because the soil was shallow. But when the sun came up, the plants were scorched, and they withered because they had no root. Other seed fell among thorns, which grew up and choked the plants, so that they did not bear grain. Still other seed fell on good soil. It came up, grew and produced a crop, multiplying thirty, sixty, or even a hundred times."

Then Jesus said, "He who has ears to hear, let him hear."
—Mark 4:1–9

Jesus drew large crowds everywhere He went, and this day was no exception. He taught them many things. He covered a variety of topics. The teaching was in parables.

As they gathered on the shore of the lake and Jesus was seated in a boat, they all had a view of the landscape. Maybe Jesus noticed, off in the distance, a farmer scattering his seed.

"Listen!" He began His parable. The Hebrew word for *hear* or *listen* means "to make a response." That is the word Rabbi Jesus would have used. "Respond!" might offer a better sense of how He introduced His parable of the four soils.

In the Palestine of Jesus's day, a farmer would carry his seed in a pouch hanging from one shoulder. He would scoop a handful of seed and fling it on the field. The fields were divided into rows.

Between the rows were paths about three feet wide that the farmer walked on to get from one part of his field to another. Travelers also used these paths. You may remember reading about when Jesus and His disciples were walking through a field of grain, and His disciples were eating some of the grain. *"At that time Jesus went through the grainfields on the Sabbath. His disciples were hungry and began to pick some heads of grain and eat them"* (Matthew 12:1). They were walking on one of these paths through the fields. These paths were packed down and hardened from all the foot traffic.

The farmer Jesus told about encountered several kinds of soil in the field he was sowing. On the surface, all the soil looked the same.

The difference only became obvious by the crop it produced. Let's discuss those soils.

Rocky soil: The farmer encountered rocky ground, such as the sections of limestone covered by three or four inches of earth, as can be found in Palestine. In those places, the roots of the plants could go down only so far. The plants sprouted upward quickly because growth was upward instead of downward. But because their root systems were shallow, providing inadequate access to water and nutrients in the soil, the plants died very quickly from the heat of the sun. This kind of soil could not be identified simply by looking at it, because on the surface, it looked just fine.

Thorny soil: Some soil had the seeds of weeds in it. The weeds were not visible, but when the sowed seeds began to sprout, the weed seeds sprouted too. The weeds were in their native soil—they owned that ground. These weeds overpowered the good plants.

Good soil: The good soil was deep and rich and ready to receive seed. It had no weeds. The soil was cultivated by the farmer, and the soil had benefited from that cultivation. It was prepared to take the seed in, let it put down deep roots, nourish it, and cause it to grow fruit.

The Rule of Four

Jesus was again using a very familiar concept: the rule of four. Rabbinic literature identified four kinds of disciples. For example, here are four characteristics of a disciple:

1. Quick to learn and quick to lose: His gain is canceled by his loss.
2. Slow to learn and slow to lose: His loss is canceled by his gain.
3. Quick to learn and slow to lose: This is a good portion.
4. Slow to learn and quick to lose: This is an evil portion.

Another example comes from the Talmud: There are four qualities among those who sit at the feet of the sages: they are like a sponge, a funnel, a strainer, or a sieve. A sponge soaks up everything; a funnel takes it in at one end and lets it out at the other; a strainer lets the wine pass through but retains the lees; a sieve allows the bran to be removed and retains the flour.

Many other writers and rabbis have used the rule of four when comparing and contrasting disciples. We are reminded of how thoroughly versed Jesus was as a rabbi of Israel.

The four soil types were all part of the same field, and three of the soil types looked the same on the surface. I have noticed certain aspects of my life that would mirror each of these soils. Read through the parable again. Jesus will interpret the parable Himself, but before we look at His interpretation, answer this question: Do you see these four soils in your own life?

Where do you have a lot of foot traffic in your heart? Can you identify an area where many people and ideas have trafficked, and it is packed down and hard to penetrate?

Where do you have a big, heavy, rock-solid hurt lurking under the surface of your nicely manicured life? Do the roots of truth grow only so far down, then are stopped by that stone of hurt?

Where in your heart do you retain old weed seeds that are ready to spring to life?

_____

_____

_____

_____

Where is your heart soft and ready for the Word to speak life? These soft areas might once have been other types of soil. How did the Lord transform them into good soil?

_____

_____

_____

_____

_____

Redeeming the Soils

If you were able to identify some areas in your heart that would correspond to each type of undesirable soil, let Jesus show you how each can be transformed into rich soil that grows lush fruit.

Hard soil: I have a friend who came to the Lord as an adult. She has experienced three failed marriages and other dating relationships that turned out badly. Her adult children are hurt and angry with her for the chaos she inflicted on their lives. Before she came to know Jesus, she tried many different paths to find God and was disillusioned each time, usually by the people who claimed to have "the answer" but were really as lost and wandering as she was. It is still very hard for the truth of God's unconditional love and His total forgiveness to penetrate the part of her heart that is packed down because of so much painful traffic. The Father has an answer for my friend. He makes this promise to her:

> *"Who endowed the heart with wisdom*
> *or gave understanding to the mind?*
> *Who has the wisdom to count the clouds?*
> *Who can tip over the water jars of the heavens*
> *when the dust becomes hard*
> *and the clods of earth stick together?"*
> —Job 38:36–38

The same One who pours out rain on the earth to soften the hardened soil can pour out the Holy Spirit on your heart right where it is least penetrable and most resistant. He is the One who created those thought and reasoning processes to begin with. He knows how to work in them and through them. Be patient. Let kingdom processes work.

Rocky soil: Another dear friend of mine suffered terrible abuse as a child and was raped as a teenager. She has a boulder of anger covered over with a shallow layer of rich, fertile soil. She loves the Word and receives it gladly and enthusiastically. She never misses an opportunity to hear a famous speaker or writer. She reads all the time. Her embrace of the Word is genuine. But she realizes that while it springs up quickly, it just as quickly fades. Then she has to find a new Bible study, new conference, or new book. My friend has deep spiritual roots in many ways, but the seed that falls on that shallow ground keeps disappointing her. The Lord has a promise for her:

> *"Is not my word like fire," declares the LORD, "and like a hammer*
> *that breaks a rock in pieces?"*
> —Jeremiah 23:29

The Lord speaks His Word into your life, and it works as a hammer to break that rock in pieces. Maybe you want big and shiny and quick and easy, but the Word that breaks the rock in pieces is slow and steady and strong. Don't keep moving on to the next big thing. Don't keep looking for the book or speaker who will break open that rock. Give the kingdom process time to work.

Thorny soil: Do you have any areas in your life in which God is speaking to you, but you are just lazy and unmotivated about responding sometimes? I could keep telling you about my friends, but maybe on this one, I'd better say, "I do." Some issues in my life require constant vigilance because their seeds still lie dormant and ready to grow again at any time. I might make a lot of progress, but then, when I feel discouraged or sad or worn out, up pops the weed and chokes out some fruit that was beginning to grow. Some kinds of obedience come right from my heart; in those cases,

I find it harder to disobey than to obey. Then other kinds of obedience require effort. The Lord has a promise for me:

> *I went past the field of the sluggard,*
>> *past the vineyard of the man who lacks judgment;*
> *thorns had come up everywhere,*
>> *the ground was covered with weeds,*
>> *and the stone wall was in ruins.*
> *I applied my heart to what I observed*
>> *and learned a lesson from what I saw:*
> *A little sleep, a little slumber,*
>> *a little folding of the hands to rest—*
> *and poverty will come on you like a bandit*
>> *and scarcity like an armed man.*
> —Proverbs 24:30–34

Every correction the Lord makes in your life is a promise—a promise that He will provide the power to obey and that obedience will yield blessing. So as He tells you that weeds grow up where discipline is lacking, He is offering to provide that discipline in you. He is reminding you that where there are weeds, the Word is being choked out. You are missing out on what He has for you. Learn the lesson. Respond! Let the kingdom process work.

Good soil: Your heart is mostly good soil. God has redeemed lots of ground in your life, making it ready to receive the Word and give the Word deep roots. Even good soil has to be prepared. It has to be plowed. When the Lord is turning over the soil in your heart, don't try to pat it all back down and make it nice and even like it used to be. Let the Lord prepare the ground for the seed He wants to plant there. *"Break up your unplowed ground"* (Jeremiah 4:3). God has a promise for you:

> *"The LORD will guide you always;*
>> *he will satisfy your needs in a sun-scorched land*
>> *and will strengthen your frame.*
> *You will be like a well-watered garden,*
>> *like a spring whose waters never fail."*
> —Isaiah 58:11

> *"The seed will grow well, the vine will yield its fruit, the ground*
> *will produce its crops, and the heavens will drop their dew."*
> —Zechariah 8:12

Receiving the Increase

Jesus told the story of the farmer who scattered his seed. Some of it fell on each kind of soil. The seed that fell on good soil made up for the seed that fell on the unproductive soils. *"Still other seed fell on good soil. It came up, grew and produced a crop, multiplying thirty, sixty, or even a hundred times"* (Mark 4:8). A normal crop would produce a 7.5-fold increase, and an excellent crop would yield a 10-fold increase. The surprise twist in Jesus's parable is the outrageous size of the crop.

Notice that the smallest crop would be many times larger than an expected crop! But although a 30-fold increase is possible, and a 60-fold increase is possible, I am captured by the idea of the 100-fold increase. If there is a 100-fold increase to be had, then I want it. I won't settle for 30-fold or 60-fold if 100-fold is available. I pray that every time the Word is planted in my life, it will yield 100-fold increase.

In tomorrow's material, we will continue to look at this parable and draw out further understanding of the process of kingdom growth.

LET YOUR KINGDOM COME

Based on what God has taught you so far through the parable of the soils, what does it mean to pray, "Let Your kingdom come"?

DAY 2

After Jesus told the parable of the four soils to the crowds, at some later time, He was alone with His disciples.

When he was alone, the Twelve and the others around him asked him about the parables. He told them, "The secret of the kingdom of God has been given to you. But to those on the outside everything is said in parables so that, 'they may be ever seeing but never perceiving, and ever hearing but never understanding; otherwise they might turn and be forgiven!'"

Then Jesus said to them, "Don't you understand this parable? How then will you understand any parable? The farmer sows the word. Some people are like seed along the path, where the word is sown. As soon as they hear it, Satan comes and takes away the word that was sown in them. Others, like seed sown on rocky places, hear the word and at once receive it with joy. But since they have no root, they last only a short time. When trouble or persecution comes because of the word, they quickly fall away. Still others, like seed sown among thorns, hear the word; but the worries of this life, the deceitfulness of wealth and the desires for other things come in and choke the word, making it unfruitful. Others, like seed sown on good soil, hear the word, accept it, and produce a crop—thirty, sixty or even a hundred times what was sown."

He said to them, "Do you bring in a lamp to put it under a bowl or a bed? Instead, don't you put it on its stand? For whatever is hidden is meant to be disclosed, and whatever is concealed is meant to be brought out into the open. If anyone has ears to hear, let him hear."

"Consider carefully what you hear," he continued. "With the measure you use, it will be measured to you—and even more. Whoever has will be given more; whoever does not have, even what he has will be taken from him."

—Mark 4:10–25

Ever Seeing But Never Perceiving

The disciples asked Jesus about the parable. He told them that the secrets of the kingdom had been given to them, but to *"those on the outside"* the secrets were disguised in parables. The phrase *those on the outside* was used often by the Pharisees to refer to Gentiles (non-Jews) and also to those who were outside their circle of learned Torah scholars. Yet when Jesus used the phrase, He was describing the Pharisees who refused to see or hear the truth.

Then Jesus quoted a passage from Isaiah, saying, *"They may be ever seeing but never perceiving, and ever hearing but never understanding; otherwise they might turn and be forgiven!"* In Jesus's day, most people knew much of the Scripture by heart, especially passages that were significant. It was common to quote a phrase or two from a passage, knowing that it called to mind the whole passage. Here is the passage to which Jesus was pointing His listeners:

> *He said, "Go and tell this people:*
>
> *" 'Be ever hearing, but never understanding;*
> *be ever seeing, but never perceiving.'*
> *Make the heart of this people calloused;*
> *make their ears dull*
> *and close their eyes.*
> *Otherwise they might see with their eyes,*
> *hear with their ears,*
> *understand with their hearts,*
> *and turn and be healed."*
> —Isaiah 6:9–10

It sounds as if Jesus was saying that He hoped the people didn't hear or understand. It sounds as if He was using parables to hide truth instead of to reveal truth. But this would go completely against everything else that God has ever told us about Himself. Would the One who came to seek and to save the lost (Luke 19:10) try to keep the lost from the kingdom?

Here is my translation of Isaiah 6:9–10, pulling in the nuances of the Hebrew text: "You hear and hear and hear, but do not respond. You see and see and see, but never acknowledge. Feed them Torah so many times that their hearts become fat. Lay it in their ears (a Hebrew phrase) so often that their ears become heavy. Spread it like a salve over their eyes until they are blinded by it. Give them every possible chance. With each refusal, they will become more blind, deaf, and unable to respond until they can't even be reached anymore. If that were not the case (otherwise), they would turn and be healed!"

Jesus said that He was proving that the situation described in Isaiah was in effect then. He identified His ministry with that of Isaiah. What separated those who were coming into the kingdom from those who were refusing the kingdom? Those who were fat hearted, heavy eared, and dull eyed could not understand the kingdom message. If that were not the case (otherwise), they would turn and be healed.

The very ones who were most smug and certain of their place in the kingdom were the ones who were proving themselves to be *"those on the outside."*

As you think through this parable, remember that Jesus was speaking to His audience, and He was speaking truth that would impact their lives at that moment, not something that had to do with the church to come into being in the future. Because it is a principle, it applies to many settings and it gives an insight into a kingdom operation: This is how the kingdom works. But it had a direct impact on that very audience.

Then Jesus explained the parable to His disciples: *"The farmer sows the word."* The farmer has to be Jesus. He sows the word as He goes. He sows it everywhere. The same word, the same message, has different effects. It takes time for the effects to appear. At first all the soils look the same. Time reveals which soil is which.

Time is required. Nothing is instant. Patience is called for. All the time that the seed is germinating, nothing is visible. Some plants spring up quickly, giving hope, only to die a quick death. It would be easy to become discouraged and lose hope. You need to know about the process so you will know how to interpret what you see.

The Word of God is a seed. A seed remains a seed unless it is placed into the proper environment. The proper environment for the Word of God is the heart. When seed falls to the ground, that which is hidden inside it begins to emerge. A little seed looks small and insignificant until it is placed in the soil.

When the Word is planted in the heart, it begins to unfold and reveal things previously hidden. All that it holds comes to life. Jesus Himself plants His Word into your heart. When it falls on that ground that has been plowed and turned over and fertilized, hidden riches spring forth, coming to light.

How can you make your heart ready, available to Jesus, for Him to plant the Word?

_____

_____

_____

_____

_____

Nothing Hidden

Jesus concluded His explanation of the parable with these words: *"Do you bring in a lamp to put it under a bowl or a bed? Instead, don't you put it on its stand? For whatever is hidden is meant to be disclosed, and whatever is concealed is meant to be brought out into the open. If anyone has ears to hear, let him hear"* (Mark 4:21–23).

He was saying, "Why would I bring light and then try to hide it?" The rabbis referred to Torah as light as of a lamp.

> *For these commands are a lamp,*
> *   this teaching is a light,*
> *and the corrections of discipline*
> *   are the way to life.*
> —Proverbs 6:23

> *The lamp of the LORD searches the spirit of a man;*
> *   it searches out his inmost being.*
> —Proverbs 20:27

> *Your word is a lamp to my feet*
> *   and a light for my path.*
> —Psalm 119:105

As soon as Jesus said the word *lamp,* His disciples recognized that as a picture of Torah. Jesus had been talking about the Word of God, Torah. Now He was saying that He would not bring the lamp of Torah and try to hide it. He was not trying to hide truth from anyone. He was setting truth right out where everyone could see it—if they wanted to. Everything that had been hidden in the Torah was meant to be revealed.

Read Romans 16:25–27 and answer the questions that follow.

> *Now to him who is able to establish you by my gospel and the proclamation of Jesus Christ, according to the revelation of the mystery hidden for long ages past, but now revealed and made known through the prophetic writings by the command of the eternal God, so that all nations might believe and obey him—to the only wise God be glory forever through Jesus Christ! Amen.*
> —**Romans 16:25–27**

What was the revelation of the mystery hidden for long ages past?

_____

_____

_____

Although it had been hidden for long ages, when was the proclamation of Jesus Christ revealed?

_____

_____

_____

This proclamation, or public declaration, was made known through "the prophetic writings." What were the prophetic writings?

_____

_____

_____

_____

Why were those things hidden for ages in the Torah now made known?

"By the _____ of the eternal God."

Why did God command that the mystery so long hidden should be revealed?

_____

_____

_____

_____

When Jesus said that what had been hidden was meant to be revealed, what was He saying?

_____

_____

_____

_____

_____

Finally, Jesus said, *"If anyone has ears to hear, let him hear. Consider carefully what you hear.... With the measure you use, it will be measured to you—and even more. Whoever has will be given more; whoever does not have, even what he has will be taken from him."*

Whatever you hear, give it careful consideration. Hear well. If you invest much in the hearing, then much will be spoken and revealed to you. When you have more revelation and understanding because you have heard well, you will be given even more. Whoever refuses to give attention to what he hears, even what understanding he has will fade away.

LET YOUR KINGDOM COME

Based on what God has taught you so far through the parable of the soils, what does it mean to pray, "Let Your kingdom come"?

DAY 3

Jesus continued His parables about how growth happens in the kingdom. He told more stories about seeds and growth. Each parable provides a different camera angle on the same truth. Growth in the kingdom and growth of the kingdom happen according to a process. It starts with a seed. It results in fruit and other blessings.

Seed Talk

Seed is a repeated metaphor in Jesus's parables. Jesus implies that a seed is what God built into creation to paint a picture of His Word.

The miracle of a seed is that it contains in it everything that the full-grown plant will become. A seed won't grow and reveal its secrets unless it is planted. Once planted, a time during which no result is observable elapses. The first part of the process of growth happens in the root system, hidden to the eye. Once planted, the outer husk of the seed dies, and the life it contains begins to put down roots. Growth is happening, but it is not visible. Only when the root system is established will the visible growth begin. The visible growth comes in stages—little by little—not all at once.

The growth that a seed produces is life that comes out of death. The seed's husk dies so that the seed's life can be revealed.

> *"I tell you the truth, unless a kernel of wheat falls to the ground and dies, it remains only a single seed. But if it dies, it produces many seeds."*
> —John 12:24

Where is the life in a seed? It's in the seed's embryo, which contains the blueprint for life. The husk, the tough outer layer that encases the seed, must be broken down so water and oxygen can reach the embryo, the life center. The outer layer must die so the life contained within the seed can emerge.

Planting the Word

Jesus Himself plants the Word in our hearts. He speaks the Word to us in His living and present voice. He is the Word living in us. By His life operating at full power in us, He breaks down all the outer casing that the Word comes in—preconceived ideas, rigid religious constructs, misunderstandings—and the life contained in the Word begins to put down roots. Then it begins to show itself outwardly, little by little.

Through prayer, the Word is planted. Jesus does His work by His Word. That is how God has always worked. *"And God said, 'Let there be light,' and there was light"* (Genesis 1:3). When I pray the Word, the Word is planted into my circumstances, and then the Word begins the process. It works out of sight at first. I would be discouraged if I didn't know the process. Then I get little glimpses of life: a shoot, a plant, a full ear in the plant (Mark 4:28).

Through an act of direct obedience, I plant the Word into a situation. Knowing the Word, but not living it, leaves the Word as seed. Plant the seed in the good soil of your heart to see the harvest. Put it to work.

In what ways is the picture of a seed an apt picture of the Word of God?

What aspects of seed and growth speak most deeply to you at this time in your life?

What word is Jesus speaking into your life right now? What husk might have to die before the life in it emerges?

_____

_____

_____

_____

_____

_____

_____

What portion of the Word are you planting in a circumstance facing you right now? If you have not yet seen the growth appear, how do you feel about the growth process that you can't see?

_____

_____

_____

_____

_____

_____

_____

The Mustard Seed

Matthew and Mark both recorded the parable of the mustard seed. Both of them recorded it in a grouping of parables. Matthew grouped it with parables about the sower, weeds growing with wheat, and leaven in flour; Mark grouped it with parables about the sower and seed and its growth. All of these parables have the same theme: how growth happens in the kingdom. Read Matthew's version of the parable of the mustard seed:

> *He told them another parable: "The kingdom of heaven is like a mustard seed, which a man took and planted in his field. Though it is the smallest of all your seeds, yet when it grows, it is the largest of garden plants and becomes a tree, so that the birds of the air come and perch in its branches."*
> —Matthew 13:31–32

In this parable, the kingdom of heaven is compared to a mustard seed. The mustard seed is the tiniest seed of all. The phrase *the size of a mustard seed* was a commonly used Hebrew phrase to refer to the smallest amount possible. Yet the mustard seed produced one of the heartiest and largest plants. If left to grow wild, it grew to the size of a tree.

The leaves of the mustard shrub were believed to help everything from stomachache to toothache. The mustard plant, once planted, was nearly impossible to eradicate. Jesus described the full-grown mustard plant as *"the largest of garden plants"* that *"becomes a tree, so that the birds of the air come and perch in its branches."* He was echoing Old Testament descriptions of the kingdom of God. Read Ezekiel 17:22–23. His Jewish audience was very attuned to hints and references from Torah. Any time a rabbi used a phrase from the Scriptures, he was intentionally referencing that passage for his listeners. Rabbi Jesus wanted those present to associate the parable with the kingdom.

In what way is the picture of a mustard seed an apt picture of the kingdom of heaven?

How is the growth of the kingdom of heaven blessing your life?

_____

_____

_____

_____

_____

_____

LET YOUR KINGDOM COME

Based on what God has taught you through the parable of the mustard seed, what does it mean to pray, "Let Your kingdom come"?

_____

_____

_____

_____

_____

_____

_____

DAY 4

In conjunction with the parable of the mustard seed, Mark records another seed parable:

> He also said, "This is what the kingdom of God is like. A man scatters seed on the ground. Night and day, whether he sleeps or gets up, the seed sprouts and grows, though he does not know how. All by itself the soil produces grain—first the stalk, then the head, then the full kernel in the head. As soon as the grain is ripe, he puts the sickle to it, because the harvest has come."
> —Mark 4:26–29

As you examine this parable and relate it with the other seed parables, consider and answer the questions that follow.

As you have been studying these parables that have seed as the main focus, how would you understand the statement, "A man scatters seed on the ground"? In your own life—right now, in the circumstances in which you find yourself—what does that picture say to you?

Write out the description of when the seed grows.

> "_____ _and_ _____ ,
> *whether he* _____ *or* _____ ,
> *the seed* _____ *and* _____ ,
> *though he does not know how.*"

What does that tell you about the seed that has been planted in your life?

_____

_____

_____

_____

_____

What does that tell you about the seed you have planted through prayer or an act of obedience?

_____

_____

_____

_____

_____

Does the farmer need to understand the process for the process to occur? Does he need to be anxious about it? Can he hurry it?

_____

_____

_____

What produces the growth?

"All by itself, the _____ produces grain."

God has created the cosmos (whole created order, both material and spiritual realms) so when the seed is planted in the soil, growth ensues. The power in the seed is released as it comes in contact with the readied soil.

Have you planted a seed that you are hovering over and worrying over? What is the Lord saying to you?

_____

_____

_____

_____

After Its Kind

The land produced vegetation: plants bearing seed according to their kinds and trees bearing fruit with seed in it according to their kinds.
—Genesis 1:12

In all of creation, living things reproduce according to their species. In reference to human reproduction, the Bible refers to the seed of the man and the seed of the woman. Humans give birth to humans. In the reproduction of plants, whatever is planted determines what will grow. When the Word of God is planted, it will produce the fullness of that Word. We will harvest the promises of God.

"As the rain and the snow
come down from heaven,
and do not return to it
without watering the earth

and making it bud and flourish,
* so that it yields seed for the sower and bread for the eater,*
so is my word that goes out from my mouth:
* It will not return to me empty,*
but will accomplish what I desire
* and achieve the purpose for which I sent it."*
—Isaiah 55:10–11

Notice that the seed produces not only bread, but also more seed for the sower. *"It yields **seed for the sower** and bread for the eater."* Each seed produces a plant that has more seed in it.

When you harvest the promises of God in your life, each promise has the seed of more promise in it. It is a principle of growth in the kingdom. *"A man reaps what he sows"* (Galatians 6:7).

Paul was echoing the words of Isaiah when he wrote:

Remember this: Whoever sows sparingly will also reap sparingly, and whoever sows generously will also reap generously. Each man should give what he has decided in his heart to give, not reluctantly or under compulsion, for God loves a cheerful giver. And God is able to make all grace abound to you, so that in all things at all times, having all that you need, you will abound in every good work. As it is written:

* "He has scattered abroad his gifts to the poor;*
*   his righteousness endures forever."*

*Now **he who supplies seed to the sower and bread for food** will also supply and **increase your store of seed** and will enlarge the harvest of your righteousness. You will be made rich in every way so that you can be generous on every occasion, and through us your generosity will result in thanksgiving to God.*
—2 Corinthians 9:6–11; bold added

Paul is taking a principle and applying it directly to the current situation. The Corinthians have given financially. A principle has been applied. They have planted the Word by obeying the command of God to give financially to the kingdom. Paul then points his readers to Isaiah by using familiar words: *"he who supplies seed to the sower and bread for food."* His audience knew those words to be Isaiah's and so understood Paul to be telling them that God would prosper His Word that they had planted by obedience.

They would receive a harvest corresponding to the amount of seed they had planted. He would increase their store of seed. They would have more seed to plant. Remember this principle from the parable of the talents: He who has will be given more, and from him who has not, even what he has will be taken away. Is that making more sense now?

Harvesting Righteousness and Praise

> *For as the soil makes the sprout come up*
> *and a garden causes seeds to grow,*
> *so the Sovereign LORD will make righteousness and praise*
> *spring up before all nations.*
> —Isaiah 61:11

If we plant the Word, then the Word will spring up. Righteousness and praise will be the harvest.

LET YOUR KINGDOM COME

Based on what God has taught you so far through the parable of the farmer and his seed, what does it mean to pray, "Let Your kingdom come"?

Matthew put the parable of the mustard seed in a collection of parables that includes the parable of the yeast in the dough. Although this yeast parable changes metaphors, it is consistent with the message of the seed parables we have been looking at this week.

> *He told them still another parable: "The kingdom of heaven is like yeast that a woman took and mixed into a large amount of flour until it worked all through the dough."*
> —Matthew 13:33

In this parable, Jesus referred to a very large amount of flour. The Greek means enough flour for about 20 loaves of bread—an extravagant amount. Even though the amount of flour is so great, still the yeast leavens the whole amount. A little yeast leavens a lot of dough.

Transformed by the Kingdom

Yeast in dough is not discernible to the eye. It is mixed into the dough and becomes part of it. Once the yeast starts its work, it can't be separated from the dough; they become one.

Yeast is a living thing. It is a fungus that acts on the sugar in the dough and creates gas as a by-product. This gas permeates the dough and is trapped in little pockets throughout the dough. It works slowly and progressively. Working from the inside, the yeast changes the texture, look, and taste of the dough. The flour and other ingredients do not expand and grow, apart from the yeast. When the yeast finishes its work, the dough is transformed.

Do you see how the yeast is like the seed? Once it starts acting, it takes its course. It doesn't require any help. It doesn't need to be watched. It just needs the proper environment.

Slow and Steady

All week we have looked at parables about growth principles in the kingdom. The principles apply to how you grow in the kingdom and how the kingdom grows in you. The principles apply to how the kingdom grows in the world. Growth in the kingdom works along these lines.

SECRETS JESUS SHARED

Look back over each day's material. Write the main things God said to you about your life this week.

_____

_____

_____

_____

_____

_____

_____

_____

_____

_____

What is the greatest challenge you heard from Him this week?

_____

_____

_____

_____

_____

_____

WEEK THREE

What is the sweetest promise you heard from Him this week?

_____

_____

_____

_____

_____

_____

THE KING'S HEART

DAY 1

The kingdom is defined by the King. Knowing who the King is tells you how the kingdom will operate. This week we will look at parables that reveal the King's heart.

Love That Pursues

Today we will look at another pair of parables, or twin parables: the parable of the lost sheep and the parable of the lost coin. Both reveal the same truth—love that pursues—but from two different vantage points.

Using Luke's record, look at the parable of the lost sheep:

Now the tax collectors and "sinners" were all gathering around to hear him. But the Pharisees and the teachers of the law muttered, "This man welcomes sinners and eats with them."

Then Jesus told them this parable: "Suppose one of you has a hundred sheep and loses one of them. Does he not leave the ninety-nine in the open country and go after the lost sheep until he finds it? And when he finds it, he joyfully puts it on his shoulders and goes home. Then he calls his friends and neighbors together

and says, 'Rejoice with me; I have found my lost sheep.' I tell you
that in the same way there will be more rejoicing in heaven over
one sinner who repents than over ninety-nine righteous persons
who do not need to repent."
—Luke 15:1–7

Luke gave us a specific setting for this parable. He didn't place it in a time context. We aren't sure exactly at what time in Jesus's ministry this occurred, but we have the scene described. Many tax collectors and sinners were gathering around to hear him.

The word *sinners* was used to refer to Gentiles or to Jews who were involved in certain forbidden trades or to Jews who were not observant of the Law. Notice that tax collectors were in their own category. Tax collectors were the most despised because they collected taxes from their own people on behalf of the hated oppressors. The tax collector became rich by adding his own fees to the taxes he collected and pocketing that money for himself. He made his wealth by extracting fees from his own people.

Many scholars think this parable of the lost sheep was occasioned by Jesus's encounter with Zacchaeus, who was an infamous tax collector. If not told exactly at that time, it was just this kind of interaction with sinners and outcasts that prompted the Pharisees and teachers of the Law to murmur about Jesus's "bad habit" of associating with society's outcasts.

Jesus entered Jericho and was passing through. A man was there by the name of Zacchaeus; he was a chief tax collector and was wealthy. He wanted to see who Jesus was, but being a short man he could not, because of the crowd. So he ran ahead and climbed a sycamore-fig tree to see him, since Jesus was coming that way.

When Jesus reached the spot, he looked up and said to him, "Zacchaeus, come down immediately. I must stay at your house today." So he came down at once and welcomed him gladly.

All the people saw this and began to mutter, "He has gone to be the guest of a 'sinner.'"

But Zacchaeus stood up and said to the Lord, "Look, Lord! Here and now I give half of my possessions to the poor, and if I have cheated anybody out of anything, I will pay back four times the amount."

Jesus said to him, "Today salvation has come to this house, because this man, too, is a son of Abraham. For the Son of Man came to seek and to save what was lost."
—Luke 19:1–10

Zacchaeus was the chief of all tax collectors. He made the most money of all the tax collectors from the taxes paid to Rome. His wealth and the opulent lifestyle it afforded him set him in direct opposition to the people at whose expense his wealth came. The very sight of him, dressed in his finery, set their teeth on edge. Among his people, he was despised and rejected—the chief of all tax collectors, but the lowest of all Jews.

Zacchaeus, it seems, had come to see what all the fuss was about. He wanted to see this Rabbi Jesus, never dreaming that Rabbi Jesus would want to see him.

The crowd, as always, was large and boisterous and crowding in on Jesus. Don't imagine a polite and constrained crowd standing along the sidelines, keeping their distance like people watching a parade. They were loud and intrusive, and they were likely following with Jesus, going where He went. In all that chaos, there was Zacchaeus—who every child attending Sunday School knows was a "wee little man"—trying to catch a glimpse of Jesus. He was ignored by his fellow Jews, who would feel tainted by even acknowledging his presence. He couldn't really join the crowd because he was an outsider. But Jesus zeroed in on him. Laser love targeted him, hidden in the branches of a tree.

Having a visiting rabbi stay as a guest in your house was considered an honor. Not only was it an honor, marking you as important, but it would also bring blessing to your house. It was a coveted position to be in—being the host of a great rabbi. And Jesus was the star rabbi of the moment.

Right at hand were plenty of acceptable, worthy people. Jesus couldn't turn around without tripping over someone more deserving than Zacchaeus. But He looked past all of them and picked out the raunchiest sinner in the crowd. *"I must stay at your house,"* Jesus said—right in front of everyone.

When a rabbi stayed in a person's house in the town where he was teaching, he very often taught from that house. People who wanted to hear Rabbi Jesus teach would have to enter the house of Zacchaeus, chief tax collector.

Zacchaeus scampered down out of the tree and took Rabbi Jesus into his house. The people muttered, *"He has gone to be the guest of a 'sinner.'"* Maybe we should call this the parable of scandalous grace. This poem from *You! Jonah!* by Thomas John Carlisle probably sums up the thoughts of the muttering people:

Indiscretion

I do not hate You, God.
Please understand.
You are O K, A-One,
the Very Best,
second to none I know,
great and beyond
my criticism so
I say Amen
to You and all Your good
intentions—but
I might be right about
Your indiscretion in
forgiving folks
gladly and shamelessly
upon the least
evidence of regret.
I think
You carry love too far.

—Thomas John Carlisle, *You! Jonah!* copyright © 1968 by Wm. B. Eerdmans Publishing Company, Grand Rapids, Michigan. Reprinted by permission of the publisher; all rights reserved.

After spending some time with Rabbi Jesus, Zacchaeus had a complete change of heart. He made a public announcement of his repentance, to which Jesus responded, *"Today salvation has come to this house, because this man, too, is a son of Abraham. For the Son of Man came to seek and to save what was lost."* Jesus clarified Zacchaeus's standing: Zacchaeus, too, was *"a son of Abraham."* And Jesus announced His own mission statement: He had come *"to seek and to save what was lost."*

This is where many scholars believe that the twin parables of the lost coin and the lost sheep and the parable of the prodigal son belong. However, whether He actually told those parables sometime in the course of this event or not, it was this event and others like it that the parables were addressing.

Jesus's detractors were especially indignant about His fraternizing with outcasts. For some, that was proof that He could not be the Messiah. Jesus turned their expectations upside down. He didn't just tolerate outcasts: He went out of His way to seek them out; He chased them down; He looked for them.

The Lost Sheep

The tax collectors and sinners gathered around Him. What a novelty for them—a rabbi who sought out their presence! Who ever heard of such?

You can imagine their curiosity and their eagerness to hear what Rabbi Jesus had to say. They, like Jesus, were aware of the murmurs of the crowd. But they were used to such. The sinners were all up close, crowded in to hear Him; and beyond them—keeping score, taking notes—were the Pharisees and teachers of the Law.

Jesus directed His attention just past the gathering of sinners to the very, very righteous ones on the edge of the audience. "Which one of you, if he has one hundred sheep...," He began. Maybe a little humor was evident in His voice. Then He proceeded to spin a story of a shepherd who has one hundred sheep but loses one. "Wouldn't he leave the ninety-nine and go search for the one lost sheep?"

Jesus was painting a picture of a shepherd who brings his herd in from the fields at the end of the day and counts his sheep as he puts them in a pen built out in the open field. His count tells him that one sheep is missing.

The contrast of ninety-nine and one was a common Hebraism. It was a way of signifying the importance of *one*. John Lightfoot, in *A Commentary on the New Testament from the Talmud and Hebraica*, vol. 3, quotes the sages as saying, "Of those hundred cries that a woman in travail uttereth, ninety-and-nine of them are to death, and only one of them to life." So the actual number of one hundred is not important, except that it communicated to Jesus's audience something in a familiar way.

As Jesus told about the shepherd searching for his sheep, the persons in His audience who were learned couldn't help but hear the echo of the prophet Ezekiel: *"For this is what the Sovereign LORD says: I myself will search for my sheep and look after them"* (Ezekiel 34:11).

The shepherd in the parable searches for his one lost sheep until he finds it. When he finds it, he puts the sheep over his shoulders and carries it home. This is a picture of tender, careful, extravagant love.

His joy over this one little sheep is so great that he can't contain it himself and has to call in friends to rejoice with him. Then Rabbi Jesus brings the parable to its close, targeting with these last words the ones who deem themselves righteous: *"I tell you that in the same way there will be more rejoicing in heaven over one sinner who repents than over ninety-nine righteous persons who do not need to repent."* Understanding the meaning of ninety-nine and one, Jesus was saying that the repentant sinner—the "one"—was the cause of more joy in heaven than were all the unrepentant, ritually righteous persons in the crowd—the "ninety-nine."

What do the parable Jesus enacted with Zacchaeus and the parable He told of the shepherd tell you about the aggressive love of God?

_____

_____

_____

_____

_____

_____

_____

How have you experienced the pursuing love of God in your life?

_____

_____

_____

_____

_____

_____

_____

_____

_____

_____

How are you encouraged to have confidence in the pursuing love of God for someone about whom you are concerned right now? Write out a statement of your confidence in God's reaching love for someone for whom you are praying.

The Lost Coin

Jesus followed the parable of the lost sheep with a twin parable—the parable of the lost coin. These two parables are two parts of a whole. As mentioned before, saying the same thing twice, using different words or phrases, is a common Hebrew literary device.

> *"Or suppose a woman has ten silver coins and loses one. Does she not light a lamp, sweep the house and search carefully until she finds it? And when she finds it, she calls her friends and neighbors together and says, 'Rejoice with me; I have found my lost coin.' In the same way, I tell you, there is rejoicing in the presence of the angels of God over one sinner who repents."*
> —Luke 15:8–10

The woman in the story loses one coin of her ten. This coin is likely one from her headdress, which would have been decorated with coins, and these coins would likely have been the only money considered the woman's own. These coins would have come from her dowry. Like the shepherd owns his sheep, she owns the coin.

Jesus created a picture of a woman diligently searching for her coin. In those days, most homes of common folk were not well lit. Living was done outside, and the house was for little more than sleeping. No matter the time of day, the house would have been dark. The woman lights a lamp, which one of meager means does not do lightly because that requires oil, which most households use as sparingly as possible. The coin is not in plain sight, so she has to sweep the house. She has to put energy and effort into her search.

When she finds the coin, she, like the shepherd, is so overjoyed that she throws a party and invites her neighbors.

Jesus was telling His audience how much the Father values these whom they have labeled as outcasts and sinners. These "unrighteous" ones are of such value to God that He stops at nothing to pursue them and rescue them and bring them home. No price is too high to pay.

The theology of the Pharisees suggested that the angels rejoice when a righteous man gives alms. Jesus said that the party in heaven is over the unrighteous man who repents.

Imagine yourself in the role of one of society's outcasts, listening to Rabbi Jesus. You've been shamed and ridiculed and judged and left out. You have believed for all this time that God has turned His back on you. What are some things you might be feeling or thinking as you listen?

Based on what God has taught you so far through the parables of the lost sheep and the lost coin, what does it mean to pray, "Let Your kingdom come"?

WEEK FOUR

DAY 2

Today we will look at the parable that is usually called the parable of the prodigal son. I want to rename it. I would like to suggest that this parable be called the parable of the lost sons. It follows the twin parables of the lost sheep and the lost coin and makes the teaching a trilogy.

Heard through the ears of Jesus's contemporaries, the parable is rich in imagery. It is a carefully crafted scene portraying unexpected, undeserved love that takes its receiver by surprise, like the love Jesus displayed to Zacchaeus.

In the two parables we looked at yesterday, neither the sheep nor the coin could do anything other than be found. Kenneth E. Bailey, in his book *Finding the Lost Cultural Keys to Luke 15*, says that Jesus portrayed their repentance as "the acceptance of being found." The one who took the initiative and put forth the effort and refused to give up was the character who represented God. The parable of the lost sons will show us the very same pattern. Read the parable in Luke 15. We'll take it a scene at a time.

Scene 1: All Is Lost

> *Jesus continued: "There was a man who had two sons. The younger one said to his father, 'Father, give me my share of the estate.' So he divided his property between them.*
>
> *"Not long after that, the younger son got together all he had, set off for a distant country and there squandered his wealth in wild living. After he had spent everything, there was a severe famine in that whole country, and he began to be in need. So he went and hired himself out to a citizen of that country, who sent him to his fields to feed pigs. He longed to fill his stomach with the pods that the pigs were eating, but no one gave him anything."*
> —Luke 15:11–16

Jesus introduced His parable with the emphasis on two sons. Both sons will reject the father and both will experience unexpected love.

The division of the father's estate would be two-thirds to the older son and the remaining third to the younger son. To divide the estate before the father's death was all but unheard-of. The Talmud claimed that a man who would bestow his estate before he died was like one who would eat with infidels. It was the father's responsibility to manage the estate and keep it safe for his heirs. When the younger son demanded his share of the estate, it was the same as saying, "I can't wait for you to die! I wish you were dead!" It was an insult to his father and shamed his father in the eyes of his servants and of the community.

Let's set the stage. In the Palestine of Jesus's day, all people lived in villages or communities. Even farmers lived in the village and went out in the day to work their fields. These communities were very compact, with houses side by side. The streets were so narrow only a single camel could walk through at one time. Most activities of the day were done outside the house, and the families of a village had continual interaction. People were involved in each other's lives and knew each other's comings and goings and personal business. Such an event as the son's insult to his father would have been public knowledge immediately. As unusual and dramatic as it was, it would have been the topic of conversation and debate all through the town. Shaming another person, especially one's father, was a serious sin.

Normally, the father, being shamed in such a blatant way, would cut his ungrateful son off and declare him "dead." The whole village would participate in a formal "burial" of the son and would be expected to treat the son as if he were dead. As always, Jesus's audience was in for a surprise. The father gave the younger son his portion of the inheritance. Adding insult to injury, the younger son liquidated it, took the cash, and headed off for a far country.

Even this act of giving the son what he wanted was an act of love by the father. As the story progresses, it will become clear that the father knew what to expect. He knew that the son would lose everything and have no choice but to return to the father's house. He would learn something in the far country that he would never learn at home. The father had to let the son "become lost" so that the son could "become found." The father had to let the son die to his love and protection, so he could become alive again.

The son wasted his father's hard-earned and carefully managed wealth on extravagant living—big house, fast car, fine clothes...or the equivalent of such—all the things he had dreamed about, all the things he had imagined would make him happy. At first, he must have been congratulating himself on how well this was working out for him. He had no boundaries. No one could tell him what to do. He was his own master. Cool!

Then he ran out of money. To add to his problem, a famine was in the land. He was out of money, and he had no way to earn money because everyone was destitute. He finally found work of the lowest kind, especially for a Jewish man: tending pigs. He was so hungry that he longed to be able to eat what the pigs were eating. Once he had dreamed about spending his wealth and making himself happy. Now he dreamed about being treated as well as the pigs were treated. But no one gave him anything.

Looking for wealth, he found poverty. Seeking to be free, he found bondage.

What was Jesus saying about the life of sin?

How might it be beneficial for a person to experience firsthand the results of sin?

As you look at this description of sin, could the son have done anything to make his situation better and rescue himself, other than return to his father?

What kept him from returning to his father as soon as he found himself in need?

What impact did his state of need have on the outcome of his situation?

Is someone you know and love living "in a far country"? What hope do you see in this scene?

We often apply this parable only to those who are completely separate from the Lord, but I find myself in a far country in corners of my life. Do you? Be specific.

At what point are you in trying to fix your own mess?

As scene 1 comes to an end, all is lost: The father has lost the son. The son has lost everything.

WEEK FOUR

DAY 3

Let's move on to the second scene, as scripted in Luke 15:17–24.

Scene 2: All Is Found

> *"When he came to his senses, he said, 'How many of my father's hired men have food to spare, and here I am starving to death! I will set out and go back to my father and say to him: Father, I have sinned against heaven and against you. I am no longer worthy to be called your son; make me like one of your hired men.' So he got up and went to his father.*
>
> *"But while he was still a long way off, his father saw him and was filled with compassion for him; he ran to his son, threw his arms around him and kissed him.*
>
> *"The son said to him, 'Father, I have sinned against heaven and against you. I am no longer worthy to be called your son.'*
>
> *"But the father said to his servants, 'Quick! Bring the best robe and put it on him. Put a ring on his finger and sandals on his feet. Bring the fattened calf and kill it. Let's have a feast and celebrate. For this son of mine was dead and is alive again; he was lost and is found.' So they began to celebrate."*
> —Luke 15:17–24

The son saw his reality. He compared it with the reality of his father's house. He thought about his father's hired men—not the servants, because the servants were part of the household and were fed and clothed from the estate. He thought about the men his father hired as craftsmen and paid wages. Even they had more than plenty.

He knew he would never be accepted back as any part of the household. That was out of the question. But maybe he could ask his father to treat him as a hired craftsman. The father's unusual response to the son's insulting demand had left the son with just enough hope to make him humble himself and take the only chance he had. The proud and haughty young man would come back a failure. The whole village would see him coming. He would have to walk down that road through the middle of the village that led to his father's house. The whole village would see him in his tattered rags and notice his dirty face and hands. The whole village would see him throw himself at his father's feet and the whole village would hear him beg his father to treat him as a hired craftsman.

He probably imagined the scene. Practiced his speech. Tried it one way, then another. He had to remind himself of what lay behind him to keep up the courage to go forward. He dreaded the moment.

The village came into view. Way out on the horizon, he could make out the shapes. As he got a little closer, he could see the people who filled the village with activity and noise. They were only specks, but he knew how their faces would look and their voices would sound. He could imagine their expressions when they finally saw him. He could anticipate the scorn and hear the words that would follow him as he walked, shamefaced, down the narrow road and made his way to his father's house.

Then comes the most beautiful part of the story: *"**while he was still a long way off.**"* *"But while he was still a long way off, his father saw him and was filled with compassion for him; he ran to his son, threw his arms around him and kissed him."*

The father had been looking for his lost son. He had been waiting for that moment when he saw the speck on the horizon. I imagine the father had scanned the landscape many times a day, looking for the son who was lost. While the son was still a long way off, before this disgraced son would have to endure the scorn and the shame he had earned, the father *ran* to meet him.

To Jesus's audience, the thought of a man—especially a respected and wealthy man—running in public was incredible. Men did not run in public. Children ran. Servants ran. Important men did *not* run. Kenneth Bailey writes that one practical reason men did not run was because they wore robes that reached the ground. Their robes were required to reach the ground. To run, they would have to gather up their robes in their hands and show their legs. To show the leg was shameful. On the Sabbath, a man was allowed to smooth out his robe, but not lift it up. The priests were not allowed to lift up their robes to keep them out of the blood when offering sacrifices. For that and other reasons, it was well understood that a proud man did not run in public.

But the father *ran*. The father ran through the village, past those who would condemn his son, so his son would not have to face them alone. He lowered himself to the form of a servant so he could run the gauntlet for his son. He endured the shame that belonged to his son, so his son could come home. He let the shame that belonged to his son fall on him instead.

When the father met his son on the hill outside the village—the place of sorrow and shame—he called for the best robe. *"Quick! Bring the best robe and put it on him.*" Who owned the best robe? The father did. The father called for *his own robe* to cover the son's shame and failure. The father's best robe was a symbol of his wealth and his stature. It was a garment that identified him. When the son walked down that road through the village, he walked it covered in the father's identity. The father's robe shielded the son from the scorn he deserved. By thoughtful actions, the father announced to all that his son was to be accepted.

The father threw his arms around his son and kissed him. He called for a ring to be placed on the son's finger and sandals on his feet. Each of these things marked that son as an honored member of the family.

Like the shepherd who finds his sheep and like the woman who finds her coin, the father who found his son had a feast. He killed the fattened calf. The fattened calf was the one being kept ready for the next great feast, such as a wedding feast. For an everyday kind of party, a sheep would be the meal.

The father invited all those who would have treated his son as dead to celebrate his resurrection. "My son, who was dead, is alive! My son, who was lost, is found!" he proclaimed. He prepared a banquet before him in the presence of his enemies (Psalm 23:5).

At that moment outside the village, while the son was still a long way off, the father found the son he had been looking for, and the son accepted being found.

What does this scene in the parable suggest to you about our Father's reaching, aggressive, pursuing love?

What does that realization mean to you?

LET YOUR KINGDOM COME

Based on what God has taught you so far through the parable of the lost sons, what does it mean to pray, "Let Your kingdom come"?

DAY 4

Today, we'll look at the third section of the parable of the lost sons.

Scene 3: All Is Yours

"Meanwhile, the older son was in the field. When he came near the house, he heard music and dancing. So he called one of the servants and asked him what was going on. 'Your brother has come,' he replied, 'and your father has killed the fattened calf because he has him back safe and sound.'

"The older brother became angry and refused to go in. So his father went out and pleaded with him. But he answered his father, 'Look! All these years I've been slaving for you and never disobeyed your orders. Yet you never gave me even a young goat so I could celebrate with my friends. But when this son of yours who has squandered your property with prostitutes comes home, you kill the fattened calf for him!'

"'My son,' the father said, 'you are always with me, and everything I have is yours. But we had to celebrate and be glad, because this brother of yours was dead and is alive again; he was lost and is found.'"
—Luke 15:25–32

Let's talk about the older son now. You know him: He keeps the rules; he doesn't shame his father; he's the good son.

As we watch this scene unfold, remember the setting in which Jesus was telling this. He was addressing it to the pious. The Pharisees were world-class rule keepers. They never met a rule they didn't like. The more rules, the better. It gave them a reliable measuring stick by which to see who measured up and who didn't. They were offended at Jesus because He enjoyed the company of rule breakers. He sought out their company, laughed with them, and even ate with them. It was just outrageous.

Jesus has a way of unmasking hearts.

The outcasts in His audience had been identifying with the younger son. Then Jesus put the spotlight on a new character. Entering stage right came the older son. The spotlight was now on him.

The older son, like the younger son, was returning to his father's house—except the older son had been away doing what he was supposed to do. He had been working hard, paying attention, getting the job done. As he approached the house, he heard the sounds of a party. While he was out working, a party had begun. He didn't go inside to see what the party was about. He stopped just short of where the audience expected to see him go. He was not about to be drawn into a party until he determined what the celebration was about.

I wonder if he guessed. Surely he had seen the father looking day after day. He, too, suspected that the scoundrel might try to come home. In anticipation, he'd been marshalling his anger and getting ready to be indignant. When he heard the sounds of singing and laughing and smelled the banquet meal, he had a sneaking suspicion.

He called a servant and asked him what was going on. *"'Your brother has come,' he replied, 'and your father has killed the fattened calf because he has him back safe and sound.'"* The phrase translated here *"safe and sound,"* when Jesus said it in real time, was probably the Hebrew word *shalom.* "He received him in shalom" would have been the likely Hebrew phrasing. Shalom means peace, wholeness, completeness, fullness, abundance. The phrase would mean that he had been received back fully and the relationship had been restored.

The older son certainly recognized by the serving of the fattened calf that the celebration was of the highest order. As the younger son had done earlier, now the older son shamed his father in view of the whole village. He refused to come in to the feast. This action was a public insult to his father, the feast's host. The rabbis taught, "It is better for a man that he should cast himself into a fiery furnace rather than that he should put his fellow to shame in public" (Talmud).

In Middle Eastern society at that time, the father would never have been expected to humble himself for the sake of the son. The expectation would be that the father would ostracize the son. He might even tell his servants to bring the son in by force. True to his nature, this father *"went out and pleaded with him."* Everyone knew. Everyone saw. Everyone heard. For this older son, too, the father humbled himself to show the son unexpected love. At the moment that the older son chose to shame and reject his father, the father had lost his son. But the father, like the shepherd and like the woman, pursued what was lost—his older son—and went out to find him and bring him back.

Listen to the older son's response: *"Look! All these years I've been slaving for you and never disobeyed your orders."* He had been *"slaving"* for his father.

He had never disobeyed an order. We get an insight into the heart of the older son...and the hearts of the Pharisees. His service, as was their service, was not out of love, but out of duty.

His words were biting and sarcastic. *"Yet you never gave me even a young goat* [the least extravagant meat] *so I could celebrate with my friends. But when this son of yours* [not "my brother," but *"this son of yours"*] *who has squandered your property with prostitutes comes home, you kill the fattened calf for him!"* The older son's heart was as lost to the father as was the younger son's in the far country. The older son was as dead to the father's expressions of love as was the younger son in the far country.

In the story of the younger son, my favorite phrase is *"while he was still a long way off."* In the story of the older son, my favorite phrase is *"everything I have is yours."* The older son lived in the middle of his father's wealth and didn't know it had been his all along. He could have had the fattened calf at any time. He could have had the finest robe, the ring, the sandals. It was all his, but he had never experienced it. He had wasted it all that time.

The father pursued both his lost sons. No matter what it cost him, he would not let either go. This is the King's heart. Love that searches and finds and rejoices—that's the kingdom.

Which "son" are you? Do you find you are a little bit of each?

In what areas of your life is the Lord directing your thoughts and inviting you to fully experience everything He has for you? Everything He has is yours.

Based on what God has taught you so far through the parable of the lost sons, what does it mean to pray, "Let Your kingdom come"?

DAY 5

This week you have been considering the love that God has for you. It is a love that is not passive but, instead, actively pursues and makes the first move. It is a love that doesn't give up. It is a love that doesn't hold your past against you. It is a love that is given when not deserved. It is a joyous and celebrating love. It is a love that surprises.

The Incarnation—the Advent of Messiah, the entering of Eternity into time—became the lived-out parable of that love. When the Torah—the Holy Scriptures so cherished by the Jewish nation—became flesh, then the eternal plan of God was put on display and enacted in real time. John said, *"That which was from the beginning, which we have heard, which we have seen with our eyes, which we have looked at and our hands have touched—this we proclaim concerning the Word of life. The life appeared; we have seen it and testify to it, and we proclaim to you the eternal life, which was with the Father and has appeared to us"* (1 John 1:1–2). That's what a parable does: It puts flesh on the eternal truth so we can see it.

To repeat, when I say the Incarnation was a parable, I don't mean to say it wasn't literal and real. God was willing to condescend to the level of our human frailties and limitations to pursue us with His love and salvation. No price was too high for Him to pay.

No matter what course your wandering takes, the King will pursue you relentlessly. Today, let's look at how the trilogy of parables shadows the reality of the parable of the Incarnation.

Maybe you are like I am, and you have been in a relationship with God through Christ for a long time. Maybe you think that looking at the parable of the Incarnation is not necessary for you because you already have repented and accepted Jesus as Lord and Savior. But I find that each time I think it through, step-by-step, sometimes from some new vantage points, I am restored again to the overwhelming joy of my salvation. Thinking about what the Father was willing to do to find me and bring me home never gets old.

Some of you are wondering if you have ever lived the parable of the Incarnation. You are not sure that you have a relationship with Christ. Listen to the Father's heart as He seeks you to bring you home.

All Is Lost

We all, like sheep, have gone astray,
*   each of us has turned to his own way.*
—Isaiah 53:6

We like our own way. In the parable of the lost sons, each son's way of breaking fellowship with the father was different, yet both had the same result. Each went his own way.

God created us for intimacy with Him. Because of sin, each of us has broken the fellowship that God longs to have with us. His complete holiness and our unholiness naturally repel each other. I often describe the kinetics of this relationship like two magnets. What happens when you have two magnets and you bring them together, north pole to north pole? They repel each other. It is just the natural way of things. You can force them very close together, but you can't keep them that way because they naturally repel each other. But what happens if one of the magnets turns around? What happens when you bring the two magnets together, north pole to south pole? The very same principle of magnetism that made them repel each other before, now makes them attract. They come together with an unstoppable force. It is just the natural way of things.

In our sinful state, we develop a warped view of who God is. We might think of Him as angry or vindictive or harsh. Somewhere deep inside, we know that is what He *ought* to be—we know that is what our sin deserves. That lie about who God is causes us to run from Him. We go our own way and end up lost and helpless.

All Is Found

Go back to the description of the magnet. When we are trying to be our own god, our sinfulness and God's righteousness repel each other. North pole to north pole doesn't work. God reaches out to come close, but there is a barrier between us that keeps us away. However, when we change directions, then we find that a relationship with God is what we were made for. We cleave to Him.

This week we have defined repentance as "accepting being found." When we repent, then we find ourselves home in our Father's house.

Remember the father in the parable of the lost sons: he was willing to humble himself and take on a slave's role just to find his lost sons. How far is our Jesus willing to go to seek us out and bring us home?

Who, being in very nature God,
   did not consider equality with God something to be grasped,
but made himself nothing,
   taking the very nature of a servant,
   being made in human likeness.
And being found in appearance as a man,
   he humbled himself
   and became obedient to death—even death on a cross!
—Philippians 2:6–8

Jesus left His position as Ruler of all the cosmos, owner of all that exists, to make Himself nothing and take on the nature of a servant. He went from the very highest to the very lowest. Like the father in the parable, His humility was out in the open for all to see. He who was accustomed to hearing, *"Holy, holy, holy is the LORD Almighty; the whole earth is full of his glory"* (Isaiah 6:3), now heard, *"Crucify him!"* (Matthew 27:22). He who had been *"clothed with splendor and majesty"* (Psalm 104:1) was now stripped naked and hung publicly on a cross.

He chose to take the role of a servant. He chose to leave behind the glory that had been His in eternity. He chose to come to where I was and seek me out and pursue me until I accepted being found. Whatever it took, He was willing to do.

All Is Yours

God has given us eternal life, and this life is in his Son. He who has the Son has life; he who does not have the Son of God does not have life.
—1 John 5:11–12

Eternal life is far more than an addendum to our life when we die. Eternal life is a new kind of life that we receive the very moment we receive the Son. This eternal, abundant, overflowing life is in Jesus, and Jesus is in us. Everything God has to offer is in Jesus.

For God was pleased to have all his fullness dwell in him.
—Colossians 1:19

For in Christ all the fullness of the Deity lives in bodily form, and you have been given fullness in Christ.
—Colossians 2:9–10

In whom are hidden all the treasures of wisdom and knowledge.
—Colossians 2:3

He who did not spare his own Son, but gave him up for us all—how will he not also, along with him, graciously give us all things?
—Romans 8:32

All things are yours, whether Paul or Apollos or Cephas or the world or life or death or the present or the future—all are yours, and you are of Christ, and Christ is of God.
—1 Corinthians 3:21–23

How do you need to respond to the parable of the Incarnation? Have you accepted being found? Or do you simply need to think on these things that you might have been taking for granted and let the Holy Spirit bring the story freshly to you? Write out your response.

Based on what God has taught you so far through the parable of the Incarnation, what does it mean to pray, "Let Your kingdom come"?

WEEK FOUR

KINGDOM PRAYING

DAY 1

Prayer is the love language of the Father.

God loves you and desires to live in intimacy with you. Prayer is more than the words you say that come sandwiched between "Dear God" and "Amen." Prayer is an openness to and awareness of His presence and His power in your life. He wants full possession of your heart. He wants you to live in the experience of His love for you.

In the kingdom, prayer is the way that kingdom resources are accessed for kingdom living. In the kingdom, prayer is the way the King pours out His love to His children. Prayer is the key to the kingdom.

Rabbi Jesus Prays

Keep in mind the relationship between a rabbi and his disciples. The rabbi is reproducing himself in his disciples. The disciple is striving to be like his rabbi in every possible way. The disciple is looking to his rabbi to impart knowledge and wisdom through teaching Torah and through the rabbi's example and habits. A disciple is both learning from his rabbi's words and emulating his rabbi's actions.

One day Jesus was praying in a certain place. When he finished, one of his disciples said to him, "Lord, teach us to pray, just as John taught his disciples."
—Luke 11:1

This would have been a common exchange between a rabbi and his disciples. The disciples had observed that Rabbi Jesus prayed often, and that He sometimes prayed all night long. Sometimes He prayed in their hearing, as would have been expected. But other times when He prayed, He withdrew to a solitary place.

Again, it was not unusual that disciples would expect their rabbi to teach them how to pray. Notice that Jesus's disciples referenced the fact that John the Baptizer taught his disciples to pray. Within Jewish tradition, rabbis were known to give their disciples "index prayers"; these were phrases that set up a topic that the person would then elaborate on. The Lord's Prayer is a list of index prayers.

The request came after Jesus had finished praying. He seemed to have been praying within the hearing of His disciples. At least they knew that He had been praying, and they knew that He spent much time praying. Since their Rabbi gave prayer such priority and they wanted to be just like their Rabbi, it was only natural that they would want to pray like their Rabbi prayed.

Think about what they were asking Him. They didn't need for Him to teach them how to sandwich certain words between "Dear God" and "Amen." They had plenty of formal prayers from which to choose. They knew appropriate prayers for each occasion. They wanted to know how to pray *like Jesus prayed*.

They weren't asking Jesus for a Bible study on prayer. They weren't asking Him in some academic way about the doctrine of prayer. They were asking Him to teach them how He prayed. They wanted their Rabbi to reproduce Himself in them, so they wanted to pray like He did.

Jesus perfectly understood the point of the request. The question followed on the heels of time He had spent praying. His disciples were wanting Him to teach them *how He prayed*. I keep emphasizing this point because when Jesus answered them, He was saying, "This is how I pray." He was not just saying, "This is how it will be for you." He was saying, "This is how it is for Me."

This week we will look at how Jesus answered the disciples' request to teach them how to pray like He prayed. He used several forms of *masal*—parables, rhythmic language, memorable sayings. You remember that parables were only one form of masal, and that a good rabbi could put his teachings into verbal formations that would make them easy to memorize.

When Jesus explained to His disciples how to pray like He prayed, He began by stating what we usually call the Lord's Prayer. Notice how it is put together so that it is easy to memorize: short rhythmic sentences grouped into subject headings.

He said to them, "When you pray, say:

" 'Father,
hallowed be your name,
your kingdom come.
Give us each day our daily bread.
Forgive us our sins,
*   for we also forgive everyone who sins against us.*
And lead us not into temptation.' "
—Luke 11:2–4

Matthew also recorded a version of this prayer outline. In Luke's version, Jesus was speaking to only His inner-circle disciples, but in Matthew's record, He was speaking to a crowd. The version He taught to the crowd was more detailed. My guess is that the disciples, being right there with Him day and night, needed fewer details to understand the concepts. Although we are using Luke as the main source for this week's teaching on prayer, I want us to refer to Matthew's more detailed account of the prayer outline, so we can see the details that are inferred in His private teaching to His disciples:

" 'Our Father in heaven,
hallowed be your name,
your kingdom come,
your will be done
*   on earth as it is in heaven.*
Give us today our daily bread.
Forgive us our debts,
*   as we also have forgiven our debtors.*
And lead us not into temptation,
but deliver us from the evil one.' "
—Matthew 6:9–13

Our Father in Heaven

Again I will remind you that Jesus did not speak Greek. Our manuscripts of the New Testament are in Greek, but Jesus did not say anything in Greek. Several places in the Greek manuscripts, the Aramaic word that Jesus used for *father* is preserved; the word is *abba*. It makes most sense that Jesus used the word *Abba* here.

Abba is the Aramaic word for "daddy" or "papa." It is a form of intimate address. It was Jesus's use of the word *Abba* when referring to God that energized His enemies to seek His death. *"For this reason the Jews tried all the harder to kill him; not only was he breaking the Sabbath, but he was even calling God his own Father, making himself equal with God"* (John 5:18).

Jesus taught His disciples and the crowds following Him that He called God *Abba* and that is how they should address Him too. "Our Abba," He said. He was teaching them this: "God is Creator, Sustainer, Most High God, Ruler of the universe, holy...*and* He is your Daddy."

The idea of God as Father was not totally absent from Jewish thinking. In my book *He Leads Me Beside Still Waters*, I share that the Old Testament is sprinkled with hints of this father relationship God has with His people. But Jesus moved it to front and center—He made it intensely personal.

> He took this thought [God as Father] that had been a stray guest, hovering uncertainly on the dim borderland and circumference of men's minds, and *made it the center of everything*. Before Jesus many good people had thought of God's relationship to men mainly in terms of a potter and his clay, or a creator and his creatures, or a dictator and his subjects. But to Jesus all these conceptions were dim half-lights, hiding as much as they revealed.... Now that new emphasis of Jesus, that centralization of this conception, was something unheard of and revolutionary; and it changed the whole face of religion.
> —James S. Stewart, *The Life and Teaching of Jesus Christ*

In the book *Christian Disciplines*, Oswald Chambers wrote a beautiful example of what confidence in God as our Father looks like:

> A dear little friend of mine, not four years old, facing one day some big difficulty to her little heart, with a very wise shake of her head, said, "I'll go and tell my papa." Presently she came back, this time with every fiber of her little body strutting with the pride that shone in her eye, "Now my papa's coming!" Presently her papa came, she clasped her little hands

and screamed with delight, and danced round about him, unspeakably confident in her papa. Child of God, does something face you that terrifies your heart? Say, "I'll tell my Father." Then come back 'boasting' in the Lord, "Now my Father's coming." And when He comes, you too will clasp your hands in rapture, your mouth will be filled with laughter, and you will be like one that dreams.

—Oswald Chambers, *Christian Disciplines*

God is your Daddy, your Papa. Rest in His presence. Be confident in His love for you.

Right now, practice calling God "Daddy." Don't think you are being irreverent. He is King of kings and Lord of lords, Creator and Ruler of the universe, Most High God, worthy of all honor and praise ... *and* **He is your Daddy.**

What is bothering you or worrying you right now? What is robbing you of peace? Write to God, your Daddy, about it. At the end, write, "Now my Papa's coming!"

Hallowed Be Your Name

Whatever situation Jesus found Himself in, the Father's glory was His goal. When times were good and the crowds were big and the people loved Him, He prayed, *"Our Father..., hallowed be your name."* And when the cross loomed on His horizon and His humanity cringed at what lay ahead, He prayed, *"Father, glorify your name!"* (John 12:28).

The disciples learned how to pray, *"hallowed be your name,"* by watching Jesus. It was not just a stock phrase to say for effect. They heard Him pray it, and they saw Him live it.

To see how Jesus was able to look beyond struggles to focus on His ultimate goal of glorifying God, read the following passage from John:

> *"Now my heart is troubled, and what shall I say? 'Father, save me from this hour'? No, it was for this very reason I came to this hour. Father, glorify your name!"*
> —John 12:27–28

What is your struggle right now? What has your emotions in turmoil?

WEEK FIVE

Draw on what you know of the Father. What do you think His purpose is? What higher good is being worked out?

Will you let your will be aligned with His purpose? Can you say, "It may be for this very reason I came to this hour"? Write your thoughts. It will help you solidify them.

_____

_____

_____

_____

Write out this prayer, and make it yours: *Father, glorify Your name.*

_____

_____

_____

_____

Your Kingdom Come,
Your Will Be Done on Earth as It Is in Heaven

Jesus prayed the kingdom of God—the active, working, detailed, specific will of God—out of heaven and into the circumstances of earth. Jesus knew that prayer is the conduit through which the intervening power and provision of God moves from the heavenly realms into the circumstances of earth.

The two phrases *"your kingdom come"* and *"your will be done"* are two ways of saying the same thing. The kingdom is present when the specific will of God is active. The kingdom is present when the substance of heaven enters the environment of earth. When heaven invades earth, the kingdom has come in that place.

The will of God at any given moment, in any set of circumstances, is always, always good, pleasing, and perfect (Romans 12:2). When you trust that God's will is positive and beneficial and fitting, then you will be praying like Jesus.

Upon God's will I lay me down,

As child upon its mother's breast;

No silken couch, nor softest bed,

Could ever give me such deep rest.

Thy wonderful, grand will, my God,

With triumph now I make it mine;

And faith shall cry a joyous Yes!

To every dear command of Thine.

Why do you think Jesus included "your kingdom come, your will be done on earth as it is in heaven" in His prayer outline?

Pray the following over every circumstance in your life right now:

Let Your kingdom come and let Your will be done on earth in this circumstance just like it is done in heaven.

What specific circumstances did you cover with this prayer?

WEEK FIVE

Give Us Today Our Daily Bread

What do you think a Hebrew audience would have been reminded of when they heard the term *daily bread*? What kind of "bread" came to them daily, enough for a day at a time? That's right: manna.

The concept behind the daily bread metaphor is this: *Give me every day the things I need for the day. Take care of my daily needs. I will look to You and Your supply for each day's provision.* Daily needs might be material, they might be emotional, and they might be spiritual. What does God provide for you one day at a time? The use of manna as the metaphor reminded them that God's supply was generous and that they could count on it:

> *Manna* was defined in Jewish thought as "the bread that came down out of heaven." So, in their history, the manna experience was when the provision of heaven entered the environment of earth and gave life, when the substance available in heaven came into the circumstances of earth, when their earthly needs were met with the riches that came out of heaven. When God provided manna, how much did He provide? He promised the people, "in the morning you will be *filled* with bread" (Exodus 16:12). True to His word, the Lord provided. "Each morning everyone gathered as much as he needed" (Exodus 16:21). Every morning, every single person had as much as he needed. Every single day, every single person was filled with bread.
> —Jennifer Kennedy Dean, *Fueled by Faith*

For what daily provision are you trusting God right now?

Forgive Us Our Debts,
As We Also Have Forgiven Our Debtors

When Jesus took on the weight of your sin and carried it to the cross, He also carried the sins committed against you. When you insist on holding on to the hurts inflicted on you, you deny the power of His crucifixion.

Next week, we will study in detail Jesus's parables that show us what forgiveness is. In next week's material, you will be challenged to pray with deepened understanding, "Forgive us as we forgive others." We'll save this section of the Lord's Prayer for then.

And Lead Us Not into Temptation,
But Deliver Us from the Evil One

The word translated "temptation" does not always mean an enticement to sin. It often means a testing or proving. I believe that in Jesus's prayer outline, He was using the word to mean testing rather than enticing to sin. God never leads us into enticement to sin, but He does lead us through—and straight into—times of testing. When we find ourselves in a difficult and challenging situation, it is an opportunity to prove what is inside us. It puts the work that God has done in our innermost being to the test—gives it a proving ground. We can ask God to filter our times of testing so the only ones we find ourselves in are those that will make us stronger.

The "evil one" is Satan. Even when he is the one who has engineered our difficulty, he has not done so outside of God's control. God has allowed only as much of Satan's scheme as God can use to bring *"an eternal glory"* (2 Corinthians 4:17).

So in this portion of Jesus's prayer outline, the request is this: *Protect us from unproductive times of testing. Deliver us from any schemes our enemy might have to defeat us.*

Are you in a time of testing right now? If so, what is being tested and proven in your life?

WEEK FIVE

Do you believe that God has protected you from any kind of testing that would have any purpose other than producing eternal glory? Detail your thoughts.

LET YOUR KINGDOM COME

Based on what God has taught you so far through the Lord's Prayer, what does it mean to pray, "Let Your kingdom come"?

DAY 2

Jesus elaborated on His Model Prayer with a parable about a friend who needed something he didn't have. As He told this parable, He was still responding to a request and the desire of the disciples' hearts: *Rabbi, teach us to pray like You pray.*

When Jesus listed the index prayers that make up the Lord's Prayer, each one was already a familiar phrase to His disciples. What revealed Jesus's heart was which of the many index prayer phrases He chose to include and how He grouped them and the order in which He placed them.

To clarify further the fine points of His prayer outline, Jesus told a series of parables. These parables were meant to illuminate and expand on His prayer outline. They revealed His prayer practices, such as boldness and persistence:

> *Then he said to them, "Suppose one of you has a friend, and he goes to him at midnight and says, 'Friend, lend me three loaves of bread, because a friend of mine on a journey has come to me, and I have nothing to set before him.'*
>
> *"Then the one inside answers, 'Don't bother me. The door is already locked, and my children are with me in bed. I can't get up and give you anything.' I tell you, though he will not get up and give him the bread because he is his friend, yet because of the man's boldness* [footnoted as persistence] *he will get up and give him as much as he needs."*
> —Luke 11:5–8

The teaching style of this parable uses a device known as "from the lesser to the greater." The rabbi sets up a truth about something of less value or importance; then he segues into the truth about something of great value. It is a style that builds toward a surprise.

Another device in this parable is the use of extreme opposites. The contemptible friend in this parable is the extreme opposite of who God is.

The Need

Jesus opened this parable with a scene that His audience could easily envision. An unexpected visitor—a friend—arrives at your house in the middle of the night. Hospitality requires that you open your home to the visitor, feed the visitor well, and make the visitor feel at home in your place. It is a matter of honor for you. This unexpected visitor would never say, "Oh, please don't bother." That would be rude.

However, you find yourself in this situation: You don't have what you need. You have a need for which you have no supply, but you know where the supply is. Your neighbor has what you need. You don't have it, but you know who does. You know where to go to get your need supplied. Have I said that enough ways?

The Supplier

In the parable, the person in need—the person receiving the visitor—goes to the house of the neighbor who has the supply. He is sure that the neighbor has what he needs.

Jesus set up this parable as a rhetorical question. Let me paraphrase it: "If you found yourself in this situation, can you imagine this happening?" His audience would have been saying, "No! That would never happen. A neighbor would never respond like that!"

Let's consider this parable in its historical and geographical context. Remember the description of a typical village, as provided in the discussion of the parable of the lost sons. Everyone knew everyone. They lived in houses built right next to each other. Nothing was private. Picture that setting, then picture this: The man in need of bread goes to his neighbor and says, loudly enough for his sleeping neighbor to be awakened from his deep sleep, "I need some bread!" Other neighbors are awakened also. You can imagine they come to their windows or peer out their doors to see what's up. Those who are too far away to be awakened will hear about it the next day.

In the story, Jesus humorously set up a scenario that would be outrageous. As He described the response of the contemptible neighbor, the audience chuckled, I imagine. It was silly to even consider it.

Jesus described a character who is outrageously stingy to make the contrast to the Father, who is outrageously generous.

As He told the parable, His audience picked up on nuance that is probably lost on you and me. The neighbor in need doesn't go away just because he has been turned down and insulted. He keeps on asking. The audience knew that the contemptible neighbor would give his neighbor in need some bread if for no other reason than his own reputation. After all, everyone would know about this episode. Finally the contemptible neighbor gives him the bread just to make him go away.

Jesus was making a case "from the lesser to the greater." If the stingy, selfish, heartless neighbor can be counted on to give bread, then certainly the Father, who is generous and loving and giving, can be counted on to supply what you need.

Boldness, Persistence in Asking

The neighbor in need (1) knows where the supply can be found and (2) is determined to receive what he needs. If he were in doubt about his answer being available behind the neighbor's closed door, then he would move on to the next neighbor and the next neighbor. If his need were less desperate, he would give up when rebuffed and go home. But he must have what he is requesting and knows his neighbor has it, so he persists.

Jesus said that the neighbor does not give in because he is a good guy, but because of his friend's boldness—his persistence. The word used really means "shamelessness." The Hebrew word Jesus might have used is *chutzpa.* Jesus was teaching His disciples that they may be bold and open with God. Nothing is too much to ask. Jesus was saying, "That's how I pray."

Jesus was making a simple point: *God has what you need and you can be sure that He will give it to you when you ask.* If you can be sure that a reluctant neighbor is going to give you what you need, how much more sure can you be that your Father will give you what you need?

In the experience of prayer, there will be times when you may feel like the neighbor in need who keeps on asking. It may seem to you as though you are being ignored or neglected. But when it feels that way, don't give up. Persist. Keep asking. You know where the supply is.

What happens when you have to persevere in prayer? Do you feel ignored? Do you feel like giving up?

What do you sense God is telling you through the parable of the contemptible neighbor?

_____

_____

_____

_____

_____

Jesus followed this parable with more *masal*. Clarifying the parable, He continued:

> *"So I say to you: **Ask** and it will be given to you; **seek** and you will find; **knock** and the door will be opened to you. For everyone who asks receives; he who seeks finds; and to him who knocks, the door will be opened."*
> —Luke 11:9–10; bold added

The tense of the verbs *ask, seek,* and *knock* is the linear tense, which means an action that started in the past and continues into the present. They would be translated as "ask, and keep on asking"; "seek, and keep on seeking"; and "knock, and keep on knocking."

Jesus had just told a parable about asking and then asking again and again and again until you get what you need. Then He gave an explanation of the parable. Notice again how He made the teaching rhythmic, paralleling thoughts. His purpose was to teach and to make the teaching easy to memorize.

Ask, seek, and knock are progressively stronger actions.

Ask

To ask is the simplest action. A child asks his or her parents for what he or she needs, assuming that the need speaks for itself. The relationship forms the basis for the request. The child has no other avenue for getting needs met except to go to the parents. It is a simple action.

The Father wants you to ask Him for what you need: *Give us this day our manna. Provide for today's needs.* If you need it, ask Him for it—that's what He tells you to do.

Seek

To seek requires effort and action on the part of the seeker. What are we to seek? *"But seek first his kingdom and his righteousness"* (Matthew 6:33*a*). His kingdom and His righteousness are the specific things we are told to seek after. Everything else *"will be given to you as well"* (Matthew 6:33*b*). We are to look for, watch for, desire, run after, long for God's kingdom and His righteousness. The kingdom of God is where the will of God is fully present and in effect. How do we seek the kingdom? By deliberate obedience to the King. Every moment that we are in obedience, the kingdom is in effect. When the kingdom is in effect, then the power of God is breaking into the environment of earth. If you seek, you will find.

Knock

Knocking implies seeking entry. To keep on knocking suggests determination.

> Knocking is an unspoken request for entrance to a place where entrance is otherwise denied. Where you have either the right or the ability to open a door, you don't have to knock. Knocking implies an intention, a certainty that you want entrance to a particular door. You want to gain access to the person behind the door. No one else will do. You have discovered the location of the person whom you seek, and now you will knock and keep on knocking until you have access.
> —Jennifer Kennedy Dean, *Heart's Cry*

The act of knocking indicates that you want someone to hear and respond to that knocking. Knocking is desiring access to the presence and the provision of God.

The presence of God is not hidden from you. He has made you His dwelling place, and He is always with you. God is always present to you; you are not always present to Him. The search is not to make God be present, but to experience His presence, to be fully present to His presence. You may feel like you are seeking Him, but in reality, He is seeking you. Your "knocking" prayer that longs for His presence is really the echo of His desire for your presence: *"Here I am! I stand at the door and knock. If anyone hears my voice and opens the door, I will come in and eat with him, and he with me"* (Revelation 3:20).

When you are knocking, it means you need someone to *give you* access. Knocking prayer can take many forms: For example, when I open the Word of God, I think of myself as knocking and asking for full access; and when I am making decisions and needing direction, I follow up on an idea or opportunity, thinking of that as knocking on a door to see if it opens. In that kind of knocking prayer, I am depending on the Lord's promise in Revelation 3:7: *"What he opens no one can shut, and what he shuts no one can open."*

On all three of these aspects of prayer—asking, seeking, and knocking—Jesus gave further clarification through parables and other forms of masal; we will look at those, too, this week.

Jesus told a parable about boldness in asking and then amplified it further to emphasize that prayer requires persistence. What does that mean to you in your present circumstances?

The Good Gift, Not Snakes and Scorpions

Rabbi Jesus continued His teaching about how He prayed, and He used some little, one-line parables to do it. As you look at these, remember that they were a continuation of a teaching that began when His disciples asked Him to teach them to pray. He was still elaborating on the prayer outline He gave them.

> *"Which of you fathers, if your son asks for a fish, will give him a snake instead? Or if he asks for an egg, will give him a scorpion? If you then, though you are evil, know how to give good gifts to your children, how much more will your Father in heaven give the Holy Spirit to those who ask him!"*
> —Luke 11:11–13

In this teaching, Jesus pointed to a parable that God created: daddies and their children. "Which of you daddies," He began, pulling His listeners in and making it personal.

With the points He made, Jesus, again, was being humorous—He was exaggerating. Would a daddy give his son the very opposite of what he needs? Would a daddy, when his son asks for nourishment, give him something dangerous instead? Would a daddy leave his son in need? Of course not!

Having painted this picture, Jesus applied His previous teaching that His disciples should address God as Abba and look to God as a daddy who loves to care for and meet the needs of his children. "From the lesser to the greater" is the teaching device Jesus used again: So if you (from the lesser) know how to give good gifts to your children, how much more will your Father (to the greater) give the Holy Spirit to those who ask Him!

I find it interesting that Jesus summed up *good gifts* as *the Holy Spirit.* Having the Holy Spirit, we have direct access to all the resources of God, the presence of God, and the wisdom of God. The Holy Spirit is *the Gift that keeps on giving.* He is One through whom all that God has for His children is distributed.

With your Daddy, you can be open, bold, and shameless. Just ask Him; He will give you what you need.

How are you feeling about God being your Daddy?

Based on what God has taught you so far through the parable of the contemptible neighbor, what does it mean to pray, "Let Your kingdom come"?

WEEK FIVE

DAY 3

In a different teaching session, Jesus used a series of parables to clarify further the kind of prayer that asks and the kind of prayer that seeks. Let's read Luke's version:

> *Then Jesus said to his disciples: "Therefore I tell you, do not worry about your life, what you will eat; or about your body, what you will wear. Life is more than food, and the body more than clothes. Consider the ravens: They do not sow or reap, they have no storeroom or barn; yet God feeds them. And how much more valuable you are than birds! Who of you by worrying can add a single hour to his life? Since you cannot do this very little thing, why do you worry about the rest?*
>
> *"Consider how the lilies grow. They do not labor or spin. Yet I tell you, not even Solomon in all his splendor was dressed like one of these. If that is how God clothes the grass of the field, which is here today, and tomorrow is thrown into the fire, how much more will he clothe you, O you of little faith! And do not set your heart on what you will eat or drink; do not worry about it. For the pagan world runs after all such things, and your Father knows that you need them. But seek his kingdom, and these things will be given to you as well.*
>
> *"Do not be afraid, little flock, for your Father has been pleased to give you the kingdom."*
> —Luke 12:22–32

In this group of little parables, Jesus addressed both asking and seeking. Matthew listed the same sayings in a group of teachings found in Matthew 6. We'll use both the Luke and Matthew accounts to get a full picture of what Jesus taught through these parables.

Ask

One of the questions people often have about prayer is this: "If God knows what I need, why do I need to ask Him for it?" In Matthew 6, Jesus stated that you do not need to worry about things, because the Father knows everything you need (Matthew 6:31–32). According to Matthew 6:8, He said, *"Your Father knows what you need before you ask him."* Yet He taught His disciples to pray, *"Give us today our daily bread"* (Matthew 6:9). He stated the need to ask in even stronger terms when He said, *"Ask and it will be given to you"* (Matthew 7:7). Don't you find that interesting? Jesus's words assure you that God knows everything you need, yet tell you to ask Him for it. Consider why God has set things up so that prayer releases into your life what He knows you need and wants to give you.

It's simple for God to meet your needs. Everything in the universe is His. Everything is at His command. The story is told of a woman who said rather self-righteously to her pastor, "Pastor, I never bother God with the little things," to which her pastor answered, "Madam, He's God. To Him, it's all little." It would be easy for God to do for you and provide for you everything you need without waiting for you to ask. But that is not how He has structured it.

Some points stated earlier this week are worth repeating here. God loves you and desires to live in intimacy with you. Prayer is an openness to and awareness of His presence and His power in your life. He wants you to live in the experience of His love for you.

Imagine what it might be like if God met your needs without engaging you in the process. You would never recognize His provision. It would seem to you to be coincidence or just the way things are. But because you have the privilege of seeing Him meet your needs in response to prayer, you experience Him. You see how He provides for you even in the smallest details. You learn that a life lived prayerfully is a life lived beyond your limits. You experience His love, His presence, and His power.

In asking, you are recognizing the Source of everything: *"Don't be deceived, my dear brothers. Every good and perfect gift is from above, coming down from the Father of the heavenly lights, who does not change like shifting shadows"* (James 1:16–17). God tells you to ask for what you need because this interaction keeps you aware that no matter what avenue of supply He chooses to make use of, He is the Source.

Sometimes God is waiting for you to ask because you will not recognize His supply until you see your need. He waits until the need is real to you. He waits until you have come to the end of your own resources—until you have tried everything you know to try. He waits for you to turn to Him as the one and only Source.

Seek His Kingdom, Not Things

Do you remember the parable of the rich fool, the wealthy man who decided to tear down his old barns and build new ones so he could store up his wealth? Jesus followed that story with the section we are looking at today and have discussed in a previous chapter. You will see that He tied the parable of the rich fool and his brand-new barns to the parables about ravens, who have no barns, and lilies and the grass of the field. The climax of the parables came when Jesus said, *"But seek his kingdom, and these things will be given to you as well"* (Luke 12:32). This is the point all the stories were building toward.

Jesus was standing out in the open, talking to His disciples. No doubt He glanced at the sky and saw a raven in flight. He pointed upward, calling His listeners' attention to the carefree bird. On the spur of the moment, He saw a parable in creation. The ravens are fed. In contrast with the rich fool, they have no barns for storing food. They don't worry about where their food will come from. Yet they never go hungry.

Maybe Jesus looked at the ground, then, and saw a lily. These lilies were hardy; they grew out in the fields in abundance, but they also sprang up one at a time in some of the most unlikely places. A person might see a lily growing out of a crack in the dry ground, with no visible source of nourishment. I imagine Jesus seeing one of those randomly growing lilies and calling His disciples' attention to it. The lilies, He said, are clothed with more splendor than Solomon, the richest king who ever lived. They are clothed by the Father, not as a result of their effort or skill. They don't wear themselves out; they just let themselves receive.

Rabbi Jesus told His disciples not to set their hearts on things. *"And do not set your heart on what you will eat or drink; do not worry about it"* (Luke 12:29). Matthew inserted something else that makes that statement clearer:

> *"Do not store up for yourselves treasures on earth, where moth and rust destroy, and where thieves break in and steal. But store up for yourselves treasures in heaven, where moth and rust do not destroy, and where thieves do not break in and steal. For where your treasure is, there your heart will be also."*
> —Matthew 6:19–21

Did you get that? *"For where your treasure is, there your heart will be also."* If you consider your treasure to be on earth, then that is where you heart will be focused. If you consider your treasure to be in the spiritual realm, then that is where you heart will be focused.

A Matter of Focus

Knowing that the things you need will be provided, you are freed to put your heart into seeking the kingdom. But that doesn't mean you don't need to work and earn a living. It doesn't mean you don't need to exercise responsibility with finances. It simply means you don't have to worry and be anxious and be distracted by the things you need on earth. Your Father knows all about your needs and is completely able and willing to take care of them. You can put all your focus on seeking the kingdom.

Seek the kingdom. Soak yourself in His Word; let your life marinate in it—absorbing its truth and wisdom into your heart. Live in uncompromising obedience to Him. Set aside a time every day for focusing on Him without distractions. Be in fellowship regularly with other believers who share your passion for knowing Him. As you keep your life open to Him through these disciplines, you will come to know Him intimately. Trust in Him will come spontaneously. Peace will be the most natural state of your soul. You will find that you have moved from *saying prayers* to *living prayer.*

I love this promise from the Book of Jeremiah: "*'You will seek me and find me when you seek me with all your heart. I will be found by you,' declares the LORD*" (Jeremiah 29:13–14). Notice the verbs. When you seek Him, He "*will be found by you.*" The verb being used says the Lord will do the "being found." As Jesus promised, *He who seeks finds*" (Luke 11:10).

Why has God set things up so that we ask Him for what we need?

_____

_____

_____

_____

What benefit is that to you?

_____

_____

What does it mean to seek the kingdom?

What benefit is that to you?

LET YOUR KINGDOM COME

Based on what God has taught you so far through the parables of the raven and the lilies, what does it mean to pray, "Let Your kingdom come"?

DAY 4

Today we will look at a parable Rabbi Jesus told that will further clarify "knocking" prayer:

> *Then Jesus told his disciples a parable to show them that they should always pray and not give up. He said: "In a certain town there was a judge who neither feared God nor cared about men. And there was a widow in that town who kept coming to him with the plea, 'Grant me justice against my adversary.'*
>
> *"For some time he refused. But finally he said to himself, 'Even though I don't fear God or care about men, yet because this widow keeps bothering me, I will see that she gets justice, so that she won't eventually wear me out with her coming!'"*
>
> *And the Lord said, "Listen to what the unjust judge says. And will not God bring about justice for his chosen ones, who cry out to him day and night? Will he keep putting them off? I tell you, he will see that they get justice, and quickly. However, when the Son of Man comes, will he find faith on the earth?"*
> —Luke 18:1–8

What is the stated purpose for Jesus telling this parable?

_____

_____

_____

What devices do you see Jesus using in this parable that we have seen in other parables?

_____

_____

_____

Knock, and Keep On Knocking

The purpose for this parable is clearly stated. This parable teaches us that we should pray and keep on praying and never give up. Why would Jesus tell a parable with such a specific focus and goal? Obviously He knew that His disciples would have experiences in prayer that would make them want to give up. He knew times would come when prayer would feel like knocking on a door that no one was answering.

Look at the characters Jesus created: two characters from the extreme opposite ends of society's order—the judge and the widow.

In Jewish society, the honesty and integrity of a judge was highly valued. The judge had absolute power. He answered to no one. He made decisions about people's lives. The judge who feared neither God nor man was likely a real villain.

A widow was one of society's most defenseless beings. When her husband died, his assets were inherited by his sons. In the absence of sons, his inheritance went to his brothers. Those who inherited the assets decided what to give the widow. They were legally bound to give her some kind of provision. She had no say. No advocate. She was completely dependent and defenseless. A widow in Palestine of Jesus's day had no voice. She could cry out day and night, and no one had to pay any attention to her. She had no way to stand up for herself.

In this parable, the widow had no resources, and the one who was supposed to be her benefactor and give her provision had become her adversary instead and was keeping provision from her. She came to the unjust judge and kept on coming to him, seeking justice from him. No one expected her, a widow, to come to a judge demanding justice. Her actions were bold and shameless. The Hebrew word Jesus probably used was *chutzpa*—reckless bravery, audacity.

Jesus set up this ludicrous, laughable situation. His listeners probably did laugh when He set the scene. He was being funny, exaggerating to make the picture clear.

The widow had a need, and only one person was in a position to move others on her behalf. She knew that only one person had the power to do what she needed to have done. She kept knocking on his door. She was not dissuaded by the fact that he did not care about her. She did not give up, because *she had nowhere else to go*. The big, powerful judge, who lived only for himself, was being bothered by a defenseless, powerless widow. The Greek word translated "bothering" is a word used to describe boxing. It means pummeling or assaulting or beating. Jesus was being witty. He described the imbalance between the two positions, yet used words that meant the little widow was beating up the judge. He didn't mean beating the judge physically, of course. He meant that she was so persistent that she finally wore him out. He gave her what she needed just to get relief from her.

The judge is the opposite of God. Jesus was using the same literary device that we have seen Him use before. If this judge, loathsome as he was, gave the widow what she needed, surely the Father, who loves you, will give you what you need.

Only the judge could move people on the widow's behalf. One of the most exciting and amazing things I have discovered in prayer is that God is able to move other people on your behalf in response to prayer. You can keep your heart and mind focused on Him, and He can move other people to actions and decisions that will accomplish His will for you, just as the judge had the power to compel other people on behalf of the defenseless widow. She didn't keep trying to do battle with her adversaries. She didn't keep trying to manipulate the situation until she got what she wanted. She knew where her answer could be found, and she just kept knocking at that door.

When Jesus referred to justice in the closing sentences of this parable, He did not mean pronouncing judgment and punishing the bad guys; He meant setting things right for the widow—getting her what she needed.

Sometimes in prayer, you will feel like the widow. It will seem like you are being ignored. If, like the widow, you keep knocking in spite of how discouraged you feel, you will find that your Father heard and has been responding from the very first knock.

Based on what God has taught you so far through the parable of the unjust judge, what does it mean to pray, "Let Your kingdom come"?

DAY 5

The result of praying like Jesus prays—learning from Him—is that you will begin to experience what He promised when He invited you to take His yoke upon you and become His disciple. You will find rest for your soul.

Jesus's prayer outline covers every aspect of your physical and spiritual needs. As you pray like Jesus, you can leave every need, every anxiety, and every desire in the Father's hands—like Jesus does.

Think about what you have learned as you have spent time this week looking at Jesus's teachings about prayer.

Why do you think His overriding theme was persistence in prayer?

_____

_____

_____

_____

How did He move prayer from being a rote exercise at prescribed times of the day to being a genuine relationship with a loving Father?

_____

_____

_____

_____

How do you think His listeners might have reacted to the fact that they could come to God boldly and audaciously—with *chutzpa*? How do you react to that?

_____

_____

_____

_____

What is one thing the Father has *emphasized* to you this week about kingdom prayer?

_____

_____

_____

_____

_____

LET YOUR KINGDOM COME

Based on what God has taught you so far through the parables and masal about prayer, what does it mean to pray, "Let Your kingdom come"?

_____

_____

_____

_____

_____

_____

SECRETS JESUS SHARED

KINGDOM GRACE

DAY 1

The kingdom of God is the opposite of the kingdom of the earth in many ways. One of the most exciting but disconcerting things that Rabbi Jesus taught about the kingdom is the secret of the way in.

Religion for the Sake of Appearance—Not the Way In

In Jewish culture at the time of Jesus's earthly ministry, the Pharisees were the most influential group of theologians. The two main influential but competing groups were the Pharisees and the Sadducees. We might think of them as denominations. Both were of the Jewish faith and shared a set of basic, foundational doctrines. But they differed on certain details of how those doctrines were to be applied to life. The Sadducees were a smaller group, and their appeal was stronger among the wealthy. The Pharisees were the ones who had influence over the most people. Jesus's teaching was most like that of the Pharisees. In fact, He once said, *"The teachers of the law and the Pharisees sit in Moses' seat. So you must obey them and do everything they tell you. But do not do what they do, for they do not practice what they preach"* (Matthew 23:2–3).

Jesus seemed to agree that the basic understanding of the Pharisees was sound. However, they had taken the underlying principle of love for God and obedience to His Law and had added to it until it became a burden to bear rather than the means to a life of freedom and fulfillment that God meant it to be: *"They tie up heavy loads and put them on men's shoulders, but they themselves are not willing to lift a finger to move them"* (Matthew 23:4). The Pharisees had developed such a complicated system of oral law that no one could possibly keep it. They themselves did not keep the whole of the oral law, yet they condemned the common people for not keeping it.

Jesus had more to say about the Pharisees:

"Everything they do is done for men to see: They make their phylacteries wide and the tassels on their garments long; they love the place of honor at banquets and the most important seats in the synagogues; they love to be greeted in the marketplaces and to have men call them 'Rabbi.'"
—Matthew 23:5–7

Jesus pointed out that everything they did was for the admiration of others. *"They make their phylacteries wide."* Phylacteries were little boxes containing portions of Torah that they wore on their foreheads and on their arms in observance of Deuteronomy 6:6–8. Jesus was observant of oral law in His manner of dress, so He most likely wore phylacteries. Had He not, His failure to do so would have been a major issue and a distraction. The underlying idea of phylacteries was symbolic, but the Pharisees had turned phylacteries into a legalistic issue and a way to promote their own piety.

"They make...the tassels on their garments long." The tassels on their outer garments were called *tzitzit*. These were worn in obedience to Numbers 15:38–40. The Torah did not specify how long tzitzit were to be, so many Pharisees made them extraordinarily long to make a show of their devout observance of the Law. We know that Rabbi Jesus had tzitzit; that part of His garment is what the woman with the issue of blood would have touched. It was believed that if you could take hold of the tzitzit of a righteous rabbi, he would be obligated to hear you.

The Pharisees, Jesus said, had turned the Law of God into a platform for themselves. They loved the admiration of others, and they plotted and schemed to be in places of honor for all to see. They thrived on the acclaim of people. They set themselves apart from others, thinking themselves to be above them. The Pharisees had a maxim that said, "The unlearned cannot be pious." In other words, anyone who did not know the minutiae of the Law and the traditions could not possibly keep them. The Pharisees scrupulously kept themselves from being contaminated by the unlearned. They had a phrase for the masses: "those outside."

Can you think of practices in your church or your spiritual life that started out as symbols, reflecting a reality, but have become legalism and have lost their true meaning? Name them.

_____

_____

_____

_____

_____

_____

Do you do or refrain from doing certain things to impress others with your spiritual maturity or knowledge? Describe those things.

_____

_____

_____

_____

_____

_____

Do you participate in any kind of religious observance that might make someone who is less knowledgeable about Scripture or church feel separated from you and intimidated by you? What are they?

_____

_____

_____

_____

_____

Do you, in any way, "make your phylacteries large and your tzitzit long"? How?

_____

_____

_____

_____

Works Versus Grace

The Pharisees believed themselves to be the ones who were assured of entering the kingdom of God. They were confident in their position. They believed they would be welcomed into the kingdom of God because of their long list of good behaviors. They went out of their way to follow the Law and to go beyond what the Law required. They believed and taught that these practices were the basis for being given an inheritance in the kingdom.

Rabbi Jesus taught just the opposite. One secret of the kingdom is that entrance is by grace.

The Pharisee and the Tax Collector

Rabbi Jesus told a parable that illuminated God's upside-down way of entering the kingdom:

To some who were confident of their own righteousness and looked down on everybody else, Jesus told this parable: "Two men went up to the temple to pray, one a Pharisee and the other a tax collector. The Pharisee stood up and prayed about himself: 'God, I thank you that I am not like other men—robbers, evildoers, adulterers—or even like this tax collector. I fast twice a week and give a tenth of all I get.'

"But the tax collector stood at a distance. He would not even look up to heaven, but beat his breast and said, 'God, have mercy on me, a sinner.'

"I tell you that this man, rather than the other, went home justified before God. For everyone who exalts himself will be humbled, and he who humbles himself will be exalted."
—Luke 18:9–14

As is the case in so many of Jesus's parables, the two characters in this parable are polar opposites: the pious, rule-keeping Pharisee and the hated, outcast tax collector. Both went to the Temple at the same time to pray.

In the Temple, sin sacrifices were offered twice a day, morning and afternoon. During the times of the daily sacrifices, the Temple would be crowded with those who had come to pray, specifically to repent. This is the setting in which we find the Pharisee and the tax collector. They had just witnessed the moving and elaborate ceremony of the sin offering. Their hearts should have been made pliant and humble by the parable of atonement they had just witnessed. They should have been acutely aware that they were able to offer prayer only because the blood of the sacrificed lamb had brought them near.

The Pharisee was described as praying *"about himself."* Some translations state that he prayed "to himself" (NASB) or "with himself" (KJV, NKJV, ASV, RSV). The Greek is very ambiguous. Kenneth E. Bailey, in his book *Through Peasant Eyes,* says that when the Greek is placed back into the likely Hebrew expression, the phrase would be translated, "The Pharisee stood by himself, thus praying...." You will see why this translation seems the most likely.

One stylistic device of a rabbinical parable is its symmetry. Jesus was using these contrasting characters and giving them parallel actions. It makes sense to see that each character separated himself from the crowd. Each was standing alone—separated from other worshippers—when he prayed. While both performed the same action—standing alone, away from the crowd—each did so for exactly opposite reasons.

The Pharisees divided their fellow Hebrews into two categories: those who kept the Law strictly were *haberim*; those who did not were *am haaretz*, translated "people of the land." The Pharisee considered himself to be haberim. One who was haberim must be very careful about coming into contact with am haaretz persons. A particular kind of contamination called *midras* uncleanness was contracted by sitting, riding, or leaning against something unclean. Mishnah states, "For Pharisees the clothes of an am haaretz count as suffering midras uncleanness." Of course, the Pharisee wanted to stand alone and apart from the other worshippers. The Pharisee stood alone because he thought he was *too good* to be among the others.

The tax collector stood alone because he thought he was *not good enough*. *"But the tax collector stood at a distance. He would not even look up to heaven, but [was continually beating] his breast and [repeating], 'God, have mercy on me, a sinner.'"*

The Pharisee offered a soliloquy disguised as a prayer. It was for the benefit of those around him. In his prayer, he listed his righteous deeds, describing them in detail so all who heard would know that he continually went *beyond* the Law. He fasted more often than was required, and he tithed everything, when the oral law required only that he tithe anything used for food. He seemed to be unaware of any sin at all in his life. Was he attending the daily sacrifice for any purpose other than show?

In contrast to the Pharisee's prayer, the tax collector's prayer demonstrated utter humility, repentance, and sorrow. The tax collector, too, was praying publicly. Anyone around could see and hear him. But, clearly, his display was not aimed at the public. His shame was proclaimed as openly as was the Pharisee's righteousness.

The typical stance for prayer was hands crossed over the heart and eyes raised toward heaven. A prayer shawl was usually pulled up over the head, shielding the sides of the face. The prayer shawl was to create a private space for the one offering prayer. The tax collector, instead of folding his hands over his chest, beat on his chest—a sign of extreme emotion. He could not even bring himself to lift his eyes.

The content of the tax collector's prayer stands in stark relief against that of the Pharisee's. "God, have mercy on me, *the* sinner" is one possible translation of the tax collector's words. The *New American Standard Bible,* the *Amplified Bible,* and other translations use the word *the*, rather than *a*, before sinner. A. T. Robertson's *Word Pictures in the New Testament* and M. R. Vincent's *Word Studies in the New Testament* agree that the proper translation is "the sinner." The whole tone of the parable has the tax collector acknowledging a difference between himself and the righteous ones around him.

The Pharisee looked at the other worshippers and thought of himself as *the* righteous one. The tax collector looked at the other worshippers and thought of himself as *the* sinner.

Rabbi Jesus concluded the parable with these words: *"I tell you that this man* [the tax collector], *rather than the other* [the Pharisee], *went home justified before God. For everyone who exalts himself will be humbled, and he who humbles himself will be exalted."*

Trusting in the Atonement for Justification

Jesus said that the tax collector was *"justified before God."* That was the purpose of the atonement sacrifice the Pharisee and the tax collector had just watched. The Pharisee missed it; he trusted in his good works and his own righteousness to justify him. The tax collector trusted in the atonement.

What do you trust to make you right with God?

Take time right now to consider what it cost for you to have the privilege of intimacy with God and to be in right standing with Him. Ask the Holy Spirit to bring it to your memory as you enjoy the relationship that Jesus, the atonement sacrifice, has made available to you. Write your thoughts.

Maybe you struggle with believing that you are justified before God. Maybe you struggle with always feeling like *the sinner*. Right now, let the reality of your atonement settle in your heart. Accept it fully. Write your thoughts.

_____

_____

_____

_____

_____

_____

_____

_____

LET YOUR KINGDOM COME

Based on what God has taught you so far through the parable of the Pharisee and the tax collector, what does it mean to pray, "Let Your kingdom come"?

_____

_____

_____

_____

_____

DAY 2

If anyone could obey the Law fully without ever once breaking it, then salvation could come through the Law. Jesus said, *"For I tell you that unless your righteousness surpasses that of the Pharisees and the teachers of the law, you will certainly not enter the kingdom of heaven"* (Matthew 5:20). As you have seen many times during this study, the righteousness of the Pharisees was built on a scrupulous adherence to a set of laws devised by men and meant to clarify the laws of God. There were laws about everything. No one—not even the Pharisees—could possibly know all the laws. Rabbi Jesus was making the point that if anyone wanted to enter the kingdom of God on his or her own merits, he or she would have to be even more careful about obeying every single law than the Pharisees were.

What Must I Do?

In truth, it is simply impossible to enter the kingdom of God by *doing*. Rabbi Jesus made this point many times in many ways. He did so again one day when having a discussion with a Torah scholar in His audience:

> *On one occasion an expert in the law stood up to test Jesus. "Teacher," he asked, "what must I do to inherit eternal life?"*
>
> *"What is written in the Law?" he replied. "How do you read it?"*
>
> *He answered: "'Love the Lord your God with all your heart and with all your soul and with all your strength and with all your mind'; and, 'Love your neighbor as yourself.'"*
>
> *"You have answered correctly," Jesus replied. "Do this and you will live."*
>
> *But he wanted to justify himself, so he asked Jesus, "And who is my neighbor?"*
> —Luke 10:25–29

When we impose on this story our Gentile sensibilities, it sounds as if the exchange is hostile. However, from the Jewish perspective, it was a lively and respectful teaching session. Rabbis most often taught in this way: Answer a question with a question. Invite further questions. Take it still another level. Throw in a parable.

The Torah scholar *"wanted to justify himself."* That doesn't mean that he wanted to defend himself, but he wanted to be justified—meaning he wanted to be righteous and in line with the Law. But note: *He* wanted to justify *himself.* He wanted to do something that would ensure that he was justified.

The Torah expert was testing Jesus, but that was not a bad thing. It just meant he wanted to see what Rabbi Jesus thought on a certain subject. His interest seemed genuine, and he indeed learned from the encounter.

His question was typical: *"What must I do to inherit eternal life?"* It was a favorite question for debate and discussion. Do you remember the rich young ruler who came to Jesus with the same question?

Notice in the question the word *do.* *"What must I do,"* implying, What must I *do* to *deserve* eternal life? Rabbi Jesus was a skilled and canny teacher. He was not going to just spout answers; He was going to lead His questioner to the answer. Rabbi Jesus knew the ideas and the theology that formed the basis of the Torah scholar's approach. He understood the slavish adherence to the Law and to tradition. He knew His questioner was looking for the missing piece—the one more thing he could *do* to be sure of eternal life.

Rabbi Jesus also understood that the questioner thought of eternal life as something in the future. The questioner believed that eternal life would start sometime in the future, when the promised Messiah comes and restores the kingdom and the resurrection of the dead occurs. He wasn't thinking of eternal life as a quality of life that could start right away in the realm of earth. It had never occurred to him that eternity could start immediately.

The Torah scholar thought the question they would discuss was, "Who is my neighbor?" but Rabbi Jesus knew that the question they were about to discuss was, "What is eternal life?"

When the Torah scholar asked Rabbi Jesus his question, Jesus responded with questions: "What does Torah say? What is your interpretation?" The questioner answered with an accepted answer: *"'Love the Lord your God with all your heart and with all your soul and with all your strength and with all your mind'; and, 'Love your neighbor as yourself.'"* This was a popular understanding. The Torah contained 613 laws, but they could be reduced down to these two.

> *He has showed you, O man, what is good.*
> *And what does the LORD require of you?*
> *To act justly and to love mercy*
> *and to walk humbly with your God.*
> —Micah 6:8

A famous story circulated about Rabbi Hillel, who was a contemporary of Jesus. Rabbi Hillel was asked, "Teach me the entire Torah while standing on one foot." Rabbi Hillel said, "Do to no other person what is hateful to you. That is the whole Torah. All the rest is commentary" (Frank Stern, *A Rabbi Looks at Jesus' Parables*).

Let's get back to the enlightening conversation between Jesus and the scholar. The early parts of their discussion were pretty tame. Everybody was saying what was expected. When the questioner gave the stock answer, Jesus said to him: "Right. Do that and you will start living right now."

The questioner had asked about how he could be assured that he would have eternal life, which actually meant entering the kingdom of God, which is eternal life. Jesus told him he could start living that eternal life right then. If the questioner could live fully all the Law—which could be summed up in loving God with your whole life and loving your neighbor as if he were you—he would be living eternal life right then. He would be experiencing the kingdom of God immediately. The rule and reign of God would be operating in him and around him right that very minute.

The questioner had one more question: "Good answer, Rabbi Jesus. That's great. I'll do that. Just one more thing: Who is my neighbor?"

Who Is My Neighbor?

The question, "Who is my neighbor?" was a favorite topic of debate. Rabbis disagreed on this issue. Although there was much disagreement about this issue, nearly all of them agreed on a few points: A Gentile was not your neighbor; an enemy was not your neighbor; and, for sure, a Samaritan was not your neighbor.

The rabbis had decided that if you were not at war with a specific Gentile or Samaritan, you were not to attempt to cause his death. However, if such a person were in danger, you were not obligated to help him.

You see that the questioner's question was not unexpected. In fact, he probably assumed that the ensuing discussion would continue on this docile, traditional course. When Rabbi Jesus began telling a parable, no one was surprised, because that was an expected way for a rabbi to answer such a question. At first, the parable was interesting and exciting, but it was staying within familiar boundaries—nothing radical or upside down. Then, suddenly, Jesus introduced the most unlikely neighbor. Here's how it started:

In reply Jesus said: "A man was going down from Jerusalem to Jericho, when he fell into the hands of robbers. They stripped him of his clothes, beat him and went away, leaving him half dead. A priest happened to be going down the same road, and when he saw the man, he passed by on the other side. So too, a Levite, when he came to the place and saw him, passed by on the other side."
—Luke 10:30–32

Jesus set the story in a familiar landscape. Everyone knew that the road between Jerusalem and Jericho was a dangerous one, along which violent robbers were known to lie in wait. The statement that a man was beaten and robbed on that road was not surprising. Jesus included a couple of important points in His description of the victim, one being that the robbers stripped the man of his clothes. One way that a person could look at a stranger and tell something about his status or his religion was by his manner of dress. This man was left naked—left with no clue about who he was. Second, Jesus described the man as *"half dead."* When Jesus said it in Hebrew, He, no doubt, used the rabbinical description "just before death." The rabbis had identified stages of the death process, and the last was called "just before death." So the man was naked, and he was in such a state that one would need to come very close, even touch him, to determine whether he was alive.

The first character to come along in the story was a priest. Priests served in the Temple in Jerusalem for two-week stretches, then went home to wait for their next time of service. Many priests lived in Jericho. This priest was perhaps on his way to serve in the Temple. He had to be ritually pure. He could not tell whether the man was Jew or Gentile. He could not tell whether the man was dead or alive. A priest had to stay a given distance from a corpse in order to maintain his state of purity. It wasn't enough for him just to avoid coming into direct contact with a dead body; he had to maintain a distance of four cubits. The listeners could understand why the priest acted as he did.

Next came a Levite. He also likely was on his way to serve in the Temple. Levites were lower than priests in the pecking order. They did not perform the priestly duties. They were responsible for taking care of the temple grounds and cleaning and storing the articles used in worship. The Levite could get a little closer to a dead body without being ritually unclean, but he couldn't touch a corpse.

For a priest or a Levite to restore ritual purity was a complicated and expensive process because it required that they purchase a red heifer, burn it, mix its ashes in water, and cleanse themselves in a *mikveh*. So, just to be safe, the Levite also walked by on the other side.

For both the priest and the Levite, the audience would assume safety was also an issue. Each of those men was apparently traveling alone on a road that was notorious for being a dangerous stretch. To have stopped to help the injured man would have put them in even greater danger.

The audience was perhaps shaking their heads in sympathy. What a shame that this man had no one to help him, but then, who could blame either the priest or the Levite? They had each done what anyone would do in such a circumstance. They really had no choice.

Then Jesus turned the tables. He brought in the hero of the story, and the hero was a hated Samaritan.

> *"But a Samaritan, as he traveled, came where the man was; and when he saw him, he took pity on him. He went to him and bandaged his wounds, pouring on oil and wine. Then he put the man on his own donkey, took him to an inn and took care of him. The next day he took out two silver coins and gave them to the innkeeper. 'Look after him,' he said, 'and when I return, I will reimburse you for any extra expense you may have.'"*
> —Luke 10:33–35

Samaritans were Jews, but they had their own brand of Judaism: They had their own temple, their own holy mountain, and their own way of worshipping. Generations of animosity had been experienced between the Jews and the Samaritans. Only a few years before Jesus began His public ministry, some Samaritans had brought human bones into the Jerusalem Temple during Passover time, defiling it in retribution for the destruction of their temple. Hatred for Samaritans was at an all-time high. A Jew would travel days out of his way to avoid going through Samaria. Get the picture?

The Samaritan didn't hesitate. He took pity on the beaten man. The concept of pity or compassion is a description of God: He has compassion on His people. He binds up the wounds of His hurting people.

The Samaritan poured oil and wine on the injured man's wounds. Jesus probably used a Hebrew word for *poured out* that echoed the role of the priests in the Temple, who poured out the blood of the sacrifices and the oil and water libations on the altar.

The Samaritan was *doing* compassion.

He put the injured man on his donkey, and led the donkey on foot. This was the role of a servant. He took on a slave's role to bring the beaten man to safety. Then he paid the price for him with the innkeeper. Whatever it cost, he was willing to pay.

In his acts of compassion, the Samaritan reversed every action of the enemy: The enemy robbed; the Samaritan gave. The enemy walked away; the Samaritan came close. The enemy left the man for dead; the Samaritan helped restore life.

When the story ended, you can be sure that Jesus's audience was captivated. You can be certain they had been hanging on every word. Then Rabbi Jesus asked the question, "Who was the neighbor?"

> *"Which of these three do you think was a neighbor to the man who fell into the hands of robbers?"*
>
> *The expert in the law replied, "The one who had mercy on him."*
>
> *Jesus told him, "Go and do likewise."*
> —Luke 10:36–37

Neighbor is a circular relationship. If I am your neighbor, then that makes you my neighbor. It didn't matter how Jesus asked the question, the Samaritan was the neighbor. The Torah scholar picked up on it right away. The neighbor was the one who had relationship with the man; the one who didn't act as if the man were dead; the one who gave of himself for another.

Go and Do Likewise

*"Go and **do** likewise,"* said Jesus. Remember that the whole conversation was about *doing*. Jesus told the questioner to go and do something that was impossible for him to do. The man couldn't change his heart. He couldn't suddenly have compassion on someone he hated. What Jesus told him to do was not possible for him to do. To obey the Law and love his neighbor would require the direct action of God on his heart. When the Torah scholar allowed God to change him from the inside out, and when that change was put into action toward those around him, he would be experiencing the kingdom—living eternal life.

The man who was beaten and robbed is the first character Jesus mentioned in the story. What did that man do through the whole story?

The man had been stripped naked. Was there any way to identify him and, thus, know whether he was worthy of help?

The man was left with no money. Could he make any contribution to his rescue? Could he pay back his rescuer?

How does this parable of the man who received compassion and the Samaritan who gave it tell the story of grace?

WEEK SIX

Based on what God has taught you so far through the parable of the good Samaritan, what does it mean to pray, "Let Your kingdom come"?

WEEK SIX

DAY 3

When the grace of the Father is given to you, it begins to redefine you and flow through you to others. The one who has experienced grace will be a dispenser of grace.

Notice through the Gospels the number of times that the questions from the audience have to do with work or doing or deserving: How can I earn eternal life? What kind of work can I do to receive this food that satisfies? Who deserves to sit at Your right hand when the kingdom comes? (See Matthew 19:16; John 6:24–29; and Mark 10:35–45 for examples.)

Unteaching Salvation by Works

Jesus was having to "unteach" the doctrine of salvation by works. The idea of working for God and earning from God was so entrenched in the minds of His followers that He had to unravel the idea from its base. He had to uproot it. It permeated everything they believed. It kept them from experiencing the kingdom of God.

Jesus told another parable meant to cement in His disciples' minds that the kingdom was all about grace:

> *"For the kingdom of heaven is like a landowner who went out early in the morning to hire men to work in his vineyard. He agreed to pay them a denarius for the day and sent them into his vineyard.*
>
> *"About the third hour he went out and saw others standing in the marketplace doing nothing. He told them, 'You also go and work in my vineyard, and I will pay you whatever is right.' So they went.*
>
> *"He went out again about the sixth hour and the ninth hour and did the same thing. About the eleventh hour he went out and found still others standing around. He asked them, 'Why have you been standing here all day long doing nothing?'*
>
> *"'Because no one has hired us,' they answered.*
>
> *"He said to them, 'You also go and work in my vineyard.'*
>
> *"When evening came, the owner of the vineyard said to his foreman, 'Call the workers and pay them their wages, beginning with the last ones hired and going on to the first.'*
>
> *"The workers who were hired about the eleventh hour came and each received a denarius. So when those came who were hired*

first, they expected to receive more. But each one of them also received a denarius. When they received it, they began to grumble against the landowner. 'These men who were hired last worked only one hour,' they said, 'and you have made them equal to us who have borne the burden of the work and the heat of the day.'

"But he answered one of them, 'Friend, I am not being unfair to you. Didn't you agree to work for a denarius? Take your pay and go. I want to give the man who was hired last the same as I gave you. Don't I have the right to do what I want with my own money? Or are you envious because I am generous?'

"So the last will be first, and the first will be last."

—Matthew 20:1–16

What did the landowner agree to pay the workers he hired first?

What did the landowner agree to pay the workers he hired second, at the third hour?

What did the landowner agree to pay the workers he hired at the sixth hour and the ninth hour?

What did the landowner agree to pay the workers he hired last, at the eleventh hour?

SECRETS JESUS SHARED

The harvest time for grapes is a very narrow window of time. A day too early or a day too late, and the grapes are in the wrong condition.

In this parable, the harvest had come. The landowner knew that this was the day that his grapes needed to be harvested. He went to the market area where the day laborers gathered in hopes of being hired. When he hired the first group, he specified a wage. The wage, a denarius, was the expected amount for a day of labor.

As the day progressed, the landowner realized several times that he would need more laborers to get the harvest in on time. Each time he evaluated and found the need for more help, he returned to the marketplace to hire others.

The next three times he went, he hired the laborers and told them he would pay them what was fair. Don't you think the laborers expected to be paid less than a full day's wage? That would be fair.

His final visit to the marketplace put laborers in the field for the final hour of the day. He did not even mention wages to them. He just said, *"You also go and work in my vineyard,"* with no talk of pay. These laborers were just counting on the fairness of the landowner. They expected little, but a little was more than nothing.

Day laborers were poor. They lived hand to mouth. Every morning they left their houses, hoping that someone would hire them. Those who were hired early in the day were elated, no doubt, when they were hired. They would have a full day's wages! What luck! All day as they worked, they must have thought about the full day's pay they would receive and rejoiced. Maybe they imagined the look of joy on their wives' faces when they arrived home that evening with a full day's pay. Maybe they thought about the debts that would be paid and the food they could put on the table. Not every day were they hired for the full day. Some days they were hired mid-day, and they received half a day's wages. Sometimes they were hired even later in the day and received wages commensurate with the amount of time they worked. But this particular day, they would get a full day's pay. How fortunate they were this day!

Gracious Boss

When the workday was over, the landowner instructed his foreman to pay the laborers. Jewish law required that a day laborer be paid on the day he performed the work. *"Do not hold back the wages of a hired man overnight"* (Leviticus 19:13). *"Do not take advantage of a hired man who is poor and needy, whether he is a brother Israelite or an alien living in one of your towns. Pay him his wages each day before sunset, because he is poor and is counting on it. Otherwise he may cry to the* LORD *against you, and you will be guilty of sin"* (Deuteronomy 24:14–15). This law was put into place to protect the day laborer because he was poor and powerless and was at the mercy of the integrity of the one who hired him.

In the parable, nothing is unusual up to this point in the story. The setting is typical—all to be expected. Then came the twist: The landowner told the foreman to pay the workers hired last first. Now, that was upside-down—a very unusual plan of action. But the surprise was not over. When the foreman paid the workers hired at the end of the day, he paid them a full day's wages! Can you just imagine their excitement? They had expected to take home barely enough money to buy food; instead, they would be taking home a full day's pay! Anyone watching the scene, you would think, would surely get caught up in the joy of the workers who, unexpectedly, were paid more than they earned.

Why do you think the landowner had the foreman pay the workers hired last first? I think it was so all the laborers could see and experience the joy of their fellow hired laborers. These laborers probably saw each other every day as they gathered in the marketplace before dawn, hoping to be hired. They probably talked about their families and shared their fears and frustrations. They probably passed along information about employers they had worked for: who was to be trusted and who was not; who treated workers well and who abused them and took advantage of them. These men knew each other and knew one another's families. I believe the landowner assumed that those hired early in the day would rejoice that their friends also got a full day's pay.

Ungrateful Laborers

Instead, the workers who were hired first suddenly changed their perception. Rather than feeling fortunate to have had a full day of work, they felt cheated that they had to work a full day for the same wages their friends were getting for less effort.

They didn't take into account the day of anxiety their friends had spent, wondering if they would be hired. While the early workers had the peace of mind all day that they were taken care of, their friends spent the day worrying about what they would do if they weren't hired that day. Those who were hired in the last hour might have been just about to give up and go home empty-handed. They were picturing having to tell their families that they had not earned any wages that day.

The workers hired early had spent a full productive day, freed from the anxiety of not knowing where their pay would come from. On top of that, they received a fair day's pay to take home, just as they had been promised.

The landowner must have been disappointed that the joy he hoped to share with them did not materialize when they saw their friends' unexpected blessing. They were envious, and that stole their joy.

Jesus summarized the parable with these words: *"So the last will be first, and the first will be last."* He probably did not use Hebrew words that meant "first" and "last" in terms of time, but rather words that meant "heavy" and "light" in terms of weight. The Hebrew words measured the value of something, or the "weight." Those who are thought of as deserving less will get the same as those who seem to deserve more. God will allow those who have always been with Him to see and rejoice with those who spent much or most of their lives away and dead to the Father's love.

Do you see echoes of the parable of the lost sons here?

How do the workers hired early in the day remind you of the older son in the parable of the lost sons?

How are the workers hired late in the day like the younger son?

_____

_____

_____

_____

_____

What is the secret Jesus is sharing in this parable?

_____

_____

_____

_____

_____

What is Jesus saying directly to you in His present-tense voice?

_____

_____

_____

_____

_____

_____

LET YOUR KINGDOM COME

Based on what God has taught you so far through the parable of the gracious employer, what does it mean to pray, "Let Your kingdom come"?

Rabbi Jesus was having a discussion with His disciples. Like with all rabbis and their disciples, the disciples were asking questions and Jesus was responding. Jesus could hear in their questions the underlying concept that had to be untaught.

Unlimited Forgiveness

Much of the discussion that occurred between a rabbi and his disciples typically revolved around the fine points of Torah interpretation. The learned and the scholars enjoyed debating favorite topics. One such hot topic in fashion during Jesus's day, forgiveness, was brought up by Peter:

Then Peter came to Jesus and asked, "Lord, how many times shall I forgive my brother when he sins against me? Up to seven times?"

Jesus answered, "I tell you, not seven times, but seventy-seven times.

"Therefore, the kingdom of heaven is like a king who wanted to settle accounts with his servants. As he began the settlement, a man who owed him ten thousand talents was brought to him. Since he was not able to pay, the master ordered that he and his wife and his children and all that he had be sold to repay the debt.

"The servant fell on his knees before him. 'Be patient with me,' he begged, 'and I will pay back everything.' The servant's master took pity on him, canceled the debt and let him go.

"But when that servant went out, he found one of his fellow servants who owed him a hundred denarii. He grabbed him and began to choke him. 'Pay back what you owe me!' he demanded.

"His fellow servant fell to his knees and begged him, 'Be patient with me, and I will pay you back.'

"But he refused. Instead, he went off and had the man thrown into prison until he could pay the debt. When the other servants saw what had happened, they were greatly distressed and went and told their master everything that had happened.

"Then the master called the servant in. 'You wicked servant,' he said, 'I canceled all that debt of yours because you begged me to. Shouldn't you have had mercy on your fellow servant just as I had

on you?' In anger his master turned him over to the jailers to be
tortured, until he should pay back all he owed.

"This is how my heavenly Father will treat each of you unless
you forgive your brother from your heart."
—Matthew 18:21–35

Talmud actually instructs that one should forgive a man for the same offense three times. Peter's suggestion was more than double that number. As he asked his Rabbi how many times he should forgive and suggested the generous number of seven, he was probably thinking how good he sounded. His Rabbi would likely be very impressed, he thought.

Jesus's answer was a surprise. Instead of thinking that Peter had gone farther than required, Jesus indicated that Peter had not gone far enough: *"I tell you, not seven times, but seventy-seven times."*

As Peter was asking the question, he had himself in mind as the wronged party. He was not considering himself as one who wronged. As always, Rabbi Jesus turned the whole discussion on its head.

If you see yourself as the recipient of grace and mercy, then you will be likely to give others grace and mercy. As you have received, freely give (Matthew 10:8).

Are you having trouble forgiving someone?

Why do you think you are struggling to forgive this person? Finish this statement: *If I forgive this person, then...*

For how long have you been holding this grudge?

_____

_____

_____

How does it feel to think about this person and the offense?

_____

_____

_____

Are you weighted down by anger?

_____

_____

_____

In response to Peter's question, Rabbi Jesus told a parable. A king audited his books in order to settle accounts and discovered that one of his servants owed him an amount so great that it could be compared to the national debt—so great that no human being could ever possibly pay it back. To pile up a debt of that size without the master knowing about it must mean the debt came from embezzlement. This servant must have been in a responsible position with access to the master's accounts. He apparently had used his position to steal from his master.

The king had this servant brought before him and demanded payment. _"Be patient with me,"_ the servant begged, _"and I will pay back everything."_ The statement was ludicrous. Jesus's listeners probably laughed at this line. It showed that the servant was not sincere, as this debt could not possibly be paid back. The servant had no intention of paying it back; he was just buying time.

It would have been unfathomable for the king to extend the servant enough time to pay the debt. The king knew the debt would never be paid. The king had the right to throw the man in prison and sell his wife and children as slaves to recover all that he could. This action would not have been considered cruel. Instead, it would have been seen as just and fair and completely within the ruler's rights.

When the king recognized that the debt could never be paid, he did the opposite of what was expected. He canceled the debt—forgave it, wiped the slate clean. In a sense, he paid it himself. He was "out" that amount.

When the servant had entered the king's presence, he was as good as dead. He had no way to pay the debt. Prison was the only alternative. Prison was a filthy and unsanitary place where prisoners were beaten and kept in stockades. A person was unlikely to live long in prison. When the king canceled the debt and let him go, the man experienced a resurrection—new life, a second chance, a fresh start.

It was not the debt that was forgiven, but the *debtor*.

The man left the presence of his master and immediately found a fellow servant who owed him an amount that could reasonably be repaid. He locked the man in a choke hold and threatened him with prison if he did not pay. His debtor made the exact same plea he had made to the king: "Give me more time. I'll pay you back." Instead of extending the mercy he had just received, the wicked servant threw his debtor into prison.

Others told the master what had happened, and the master called the wicked servant back in. *"In anger his master turned him over to the jailers to be tortured, until he should pay back all he owed."*

Forgiven to Forgive

Choosing not to forgive others is closing the door to God's forgiveness. This does not mean that when you do not forgive, God withholds His forgiveness as a punishment. It does not mean that you earn your forgiveness by forgiving others. If this were so, it would directly contradict the entire gospel message. Your forgiveness is a settled matter—settled at the cross. Christ's death in your place fulfilled your obligation and erased your debt. God will not go back on His Word. Yet this concept—that our forgiveness of those who wrong us is tied to God's forgiveness of us—is repeated and emphasized by Jesus. So we must come to an understanding of what it means.

Foundational to this understanding is the recognition of how much God has forgiven you. If you were the only person ever to commit a sin, Jesus would still have died for you. It still would have taken His death on the cross to pay for your sins alone. When He died on the cross, it was for your sins. The Father has forgiven you more than you will ever be called upon to forgive any other person. The cost of His forgiveness is a higher price than you will ever have to pay. No matter what anyone has ever done to you, that person's sin against you does not come close to the measure of your sins against God.

Second, you are not the one who does the forgiving. The Father living in you does His work (John 14:10). You, on your own, have neither the inclination nor the ability to forgive. You are the conduit of His forgiveness. Holding on to anger cuts off the flow of His power through you. It clogs the channel through which His love flows.

Third, understand that when Jesus said, *"So that your Father in heaven may forgive you your sins"* (Mark 11:25), He did not refer to the action of forgiving—which Jesus knew would be finished at the cross—but instead referred to having His forgiveness in your experience. He wants forgiveness to move from being an abstract theological concept to being your truth. Deliberately nursing a grievance, holding it close and giving it nourishment, keeps the reality of the Father's forgiveness from you. When you choose to hold on to anger or bitterness, you refuse to let go of a sin—the sin of unforgiveness. Confessing and turning from a sin are the actions that bring the Father's forgiveness into your experience.

The Scripture tells us that deliberate unforgiveness gives the enemy an opening. Paul wrote, *"What I have forgiven—if there was anything to forgive— I have forgiven in the sight of Christ for your sake, in order that Satan might not outwit us. For we are not unaware of his schemes"* (2 Corinthians 2:10–11). As you forgive those who have wronged you, you close the door to Satan's schemes and you open the door to the power of God.

You can have the peace that comes from forgiving others and letting go of the turmoil that anger and resentment bring to your emotions. When you believe what God says about the high price of your forgiveness, you will be ready to forgive anybody anything. Forgive and let the peace of Christ stand guard over your heart.

When you choose not to forgive, then your angry thoughts and raging emotions become your "torturers" and you are imprisoned in your own bitterness.

What does refusing to forgive do to you?

_____

_____

_____

_____

_____

_____

Why does your loving Father want you to forgive others?

_____

_____

_____

_____

_____

_____

Unforgiveness hurts you, not your offender. I've heard it said that holding on to anger is like drinking poison and hoping it kills someone else. Unforgiveness makes no sense.

Burdens Not Yours to Bear

You were not designed to carry anger and bitterness. Doing so weighs you down and holds you back. Because the Father loves you, He does not want you bearing a burden that is not yours to bear.

Let me repeat something from last week: When Jesus took on the weight of your sin and carried it to the cross, He also carried the sins committed against you. When you insist on holding on to the hurts inflicted on you, you deny the power of His crucifixion. He died for sinners, for the ungodly. *"You see, at just the right time, when we were still powerless, Christ died for the ungodly.... God demonstrates his own love for us in this: While we were still sinners, Christ died for us"* (Romans 5:6, 8). Is your offender a sinner? Christ died for his sins. Is your offender ungodly? Christ died for her. Extend grace—the same grace that God extended to you.

Not only did He carry your sin, but He bore the weight of your grief and your sorrows. He bore the hurt of the sins committed against you. Just as you have leaned the weight of your sins on Him, now lean the weight of your grief and your sorrow on Him. Let Him carry it. It is too heavy for you.

By bearing the weight of your own hurt, you allow the offense to continue and to multiply its effect on you. You may be passing the hurt along to others in your life. The offense grows and spreads. *"See to it that no one misses the grace of God and that no bitter root grows up to cause trouble and defile many"* (Hebrews 12:15). If bitterness is allowed to take root in you, it will begin to grow fruit. Your actions, words, attitudes, and responses will be bitter fruit growing from a bitter root. It will create bitterness in those who are exposed to it. One offense can poison many people, even spreading from generation to generation. Do you really want to enable your offender to have access to so many lives? Wouldn't it be better to forgive and let your life produce the fruit of the Spirit instead?

LET YOUR KINGDOM COME

Based on what God has taught you so far through the parable of the wicked servant, what does it mean to pray, "Let Your kingdom come"?

On a certain Sabbath, Jesus had perhaps been the visiting rabbi in the synagogue. He may have been called upon to read the portion of Holy Scripture for the day and then to expound on it. A Pharisee named Simon invited the visiting rabbi to his house for a meal. During the meal, a woman with a bad reputation—maybe a prostitute—came in, bringing an alabaster jar of costly ointment. Weeping, she wet Jesus's feet with her tears, wiped them with her hair, kissed them, and anointed them with perfume. Read this touching story from Luke:

> *Now one of the Pharisees invited Jesus to have dinner with him, so he went to the Pharisee's house and reclined at the table. When a woman who had lived a sinful life in that town learned that Jesus was eating at the Pharisee's house, she brought an alabaster jar of perfume, and as she stood behind him at his feet weeping, she began to wet his feet with her tears. Then she wiped them with her hair, kissed them and poured perfume on them.*
>
> *When the Pharisee who had invited him saw this, he said to himself, "If this man were a prophet, he would know who is touching him and what kind of woman she is—that she is a sinner."*
>
> *Jesus answered him, "Simon, I have something to tell you."*
>
> *"Tell me, teacher," he said.*
>
> *"Two men owed money to a certain moneylender. One owed him five hundred denarii, and the other fifty. Neither of them had the money to pay him back, so he canceled the debts of both. Now which of them will love him more?"*
>
> *Simon replied, "I suppose the one who had the bigger debt canceled."*
>
> *"You have judged correctly," Jesus said.*
>
> *Then he turned toward the woman and said to Simon, "Do you see this woman? I came into your house. You did not give me any water for my feet, but she wet my feet with her tears and wiped them with her hair. You did not give me a kiss, but this woman, from the time I entered, has not stopped kissing my feet. You did not put oil on my head, but she has poured perfume on my feet. Therefore, I tell you, her many sins have been*

forgiven—for she loved much. But he who has been forgiven little loves little."

Then Jesus said to her, "Your sins are forgiven."

—Luke 7:36–48

The houses in Palestine were very open. It was not unusual for someone off the street to come right into a wealthy man's house during mealtime to beg for food. You notice that no one threw out this woman. Her presence was not so unusual, but her actions *were*.

She was acting out part of a parable. Jesus told the parable she was enacting: There were two debtors. One owed much, and the other owed a little. When the moneylender canceled (forgave) both debts, which debtor loved him more? Not a hard question.

Then Jesus pointed out that Simon had not shown Him any love when He came in his house. Simon did not believe himself to be in need of forgiveness. But this woman knew that she had experienced a resurrection. She had been lost, but now she was found. She had been dead, but now she was alive. So she poured out a costly anointing on the body of Christ.

She was acting out another parable that soon would be enacted in reality. The days were fast approaching when Jesus would pour out a costly anointing. Like the alabaster jar, His body would be broken so the anointing could be poured out.

The forgiveness we receive from the Father is not a passive act but, instead, is a costly transaction.

The Greek word translated "forgive" means "to send off" or "to send away." The act of forgiving separates the sin from the one who sinned. It sends away the sin, with its penalty and its attendant guilt. This transaction was pictured in the Old Testament by the sacrificial system. The guilty person made a sin offering or guilt offering with an unblemished animal from his own livestock. Before killing the animal, he laid his hands on the animal. He leaned into the animal with all his weight. This symbolized laying his sins on the animal; the animal was bearing the "weight" of his sins. Then he killed the animal, recognizing that the payment for sin is death. As that person leaned his weight upon the sacrificial animal, Yahweh declared, *"It will be accepted on his behalf to make atonement for him"* (Leviticus 1:4). The sin was separated from the one who sinned because it was placed on the sacrifice.

Forgiveness from the Father is available for you and me because *"the LORD has laid on him* [Jesus] *the iniquity of us all"* (Isaiah 53:6).

Do you see? God separated your sin from you. He took the sin off of you and placed it on the Son. He sent your sin away. The One who knew no sin became sin for us. It is finished and settled. Lean the weight of your sin on Him who took your sin to the cross. You are forgiven much. Love much.

Loved Much

He took on the time and space constraints of earth,
Let a veil of flesh conceal His worth,
Set redemption's plan in motion with His birth.

It was for me.
It was for me

He gave up His flesh—an offering for my sin,
Let God's wrath toward me be spent on Him,
Poured out His life so my life could begin.

It was for me.
It was for me

He threw off the time and space constraints of earth,
Shed His veil of flesh, revealed His worth,
Opened up for me the way to Spirit birth.

It was for me.
—© Jennifer Kennedy Dean

How much He loves you! The act of sacrifice—the sacrifice of the Son and the sacrifice of the Father—was not a generic, impersonal action, but a specific, directed, intimate action on your behalf. The Father's love for you is as personal as if you were His only love.

Consider the cost of your salvation and the love that was poured out at the cross to set you free. Write your thoughts, directing them to the living Jesus.

WEEK SIX

LET YOUR KINGDOM COME

Based on what God has taught you so far through the parable of the two debtors, what does it mean to pray, "Let Your kingdom come"?

CLOSING COMMENTS FROM JENNIFER

My prayer is that as you have journeyed with Rabbi Jesus through His parables, you have come to a deeper intimacy with Him. I hope you have come to see Him as personable and winsome. I hope you are learning to enjoy His company more and more.

He wants to keep revealing the secrets of the kingdom to you. He wants to keep teaching you the hidden depths in His Word. He wants to keep being your Rabbi—every day, every hour, every minute.

The King wants you as His confidant—one who knows His secrets. He for whom all the morning stars sing, He who is the Lodestar of all history and the Linchpin of all creation, wants you to know His secrets.

Learn from Him how to live fully in the kingdom. Let Him daily teach you how to access the kingdom's power and provision for your life. Keep asking Rabbi Jesus, "Rabbi, right now, in this moment and under these circumstances, show me the kingdom. Right now, in this conversation and in this interaction, let Your kingdom come. Right now, in the midst of this need, reveal the kingdom. Rabbi Jesus, when You look at what I'm looking at, what do You see?" Be a disciple of your Rabbi.

Watch for the parables with which the Father surrounds you—those parables that He works into the fabric of your life. Keep your eyes focused on spiritual reality cast in earthly forms. Live with an alertness to the Spirit's gusts, which blow when least expected. Throw out the old wineskins, and get ready for the new wine. Live *"with your cloak tucked into your belt, your sandals on your feet and your staff in your hand"* (Exodus 12:11)—ready, anywhere, anytime, when the call comes.

Cover yourself with the dust of your Rabbi's feet.

TO SCHEDULE

Jennifer Kennedy Dean

FOR YOUR EVENT, CONTACT:

The Praying Life Foundation
P. O. Box 1113
Blue Springs, MO 64013
888-844-6647
seminars@prayinglife.org
www.prayinglife.org

Visit www.prayinglife.org:

- Find answers to frequently asked questions.
- Ask Jennifer your own questions.
- Find a monthly column by Jennifer Kennedy Dean.
- Discover a wealth of resources for your praying life.

STUDIES AND BOOKS BY
Jennifer

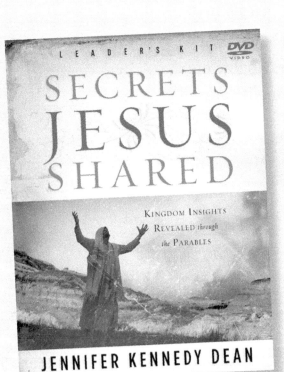

Secrets Jesus Shared Leader Kit
UPC: 8446250-1073-6
ISBN-10: 1-59669-113-1
ISBN-13: 978-1-59669-113-1

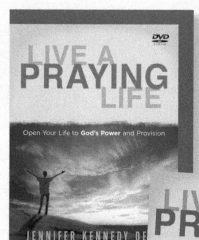

Live a Praying Life Leader Kit

UPC: 8446250-1012-5
ISBN-10: 1-59669-020-8
ISBN-13: 978-1-59669-020-2

Live a Praying Life
Open Your Life to God's Power and Provision

ISBN-10: 1-56309-752-4
ISBN-13: 978-1-56309-752-2

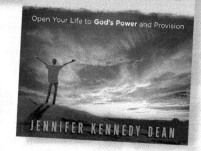

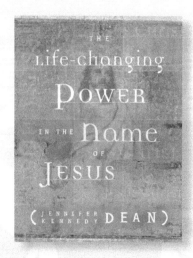

The Life-Changing Power in the Name of Jesus

ISBN-10: 1-56309-841-5
ISBN-13: 978-1-56309-841-3

The Life-Changing Power in the Blood of Christ

ISBN-10: 1-56309-753-2
ISBN-13: 978-1-56309-753-9

Heart's Cry
Principles of Prayer, Revised Edition
ISBN-10: 1-59669-095-X
ISBN-13: 978-1-59669-095-0

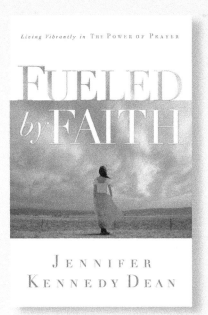

Fueled by Faith
Living Vibrantly in the Power of Prayer
ISBN-10: 1-56309-993-4
ISBN-13: 978-1-56309-993-9

Legacy of Prayer
A Spiritual Trust Fund for the Generations
ISBN-10: 1-56309-711-7
ISBN-13: 978-1-56309-711-9

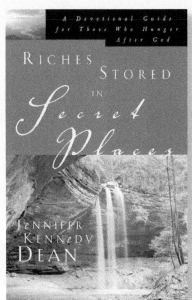

Riches Stored in Secret Places
*A Devotional Guide for Those
Who Hunger After God*
ISBN-10: 1-56309-203-4
ISBN-13: 978-1-56309-203-9

New Hope® Publishers is a division of WMU®,
an international organization that challenges Christian believers
to understand and be radically involved in God's mission.
For more information about WMU, go to www.wmu.com.
More information about New Hope books may be found
at www.newhopepublishers.com. New Hope books
may be purchased at your local bookstore.